SACRED ROME

SACRED ROME

MONDADORI

© 1999 Arnoldo Mondadori S.p.A., Milan
Pilgrims in Rome
Revised second edition
© 2012 Mondadori Electa S.p.A., Milan

First edition published by:
Fabio Ratti Editoria srl, via Medici 13, 20123 Milan

Authors of the texts: Nicolò Cesta (San Paolo fuori le mura); Alessandro De Angelis
(Homes of the Saints); Carmelo Dotolo (Places of Worship of Other Churches and Religious
Communities); Raffaella Giuliani (Catacombs or Sanctuaries of the Martyrs, Historic
Churches); Luca Mariani (San Giovanni in Laterano, Historic Churches); Danilo Mazzoleni
(San Pietro in Vaticano, Santa Maria Maggiore, San Lorenzo fuori le mura, Santa Pudenziana,
San Clemente, Historic Churches); Mario Sensi (History of Rome, Sancta Sanctorum and Holy
Stairs, Santa Croce in Gerusalemme).
Editorial coordination: Vito Mancuso

Editing: Barbara Cacciani, Giovanni Francesio, Laura Ricordati
Layout: Oriana Bianchetti, Stefania Testa, Silvia Tomasone
Readers and revisors: Filippo Catalano, Enrico dal Covolo

Publication of the second edition
Graphic design: Eva Volpato
Layout: Elisa Seghezzi
Editing: Federica Tuzzi
Translations: Sylvia Notini

ISBN: 978883708979-5

Printed in February 2012 at Mondadori Printing S.p.A., Verona
Printed in Italy

The information contained in this book was updated as accurately as possible at the time of its
printing. Nonetheless, the publisher makes no warranty about the accuracy or completeness of
the information: telephone numbers, opening hours, prices, works on display at the museums,
and other similar information are all subject to change. The publisher thus disclaims all liability
arising from the use of this guidebook.
Any observations or suggestions can be sent to the publisher who will see that they are taken
into account should there be a future edition of the book.
Observations or suggestions can be sent to: Geo Mondadori – via Trentacoste, 7 – 20134 Milan
– fax 02 21563262 www.geomondadori.com

Front cover: Gian Lorenzo Bernini, *Angel with Scroll* (1669). Ponte Sant'Angelo
On page 2: Caravaggio, *Madonna di Loreto* (1603-1605). Church of Sant'Agostino
On pages 18-19: Antoniazzo Romano, *The Invention of the Holy* Cross (ca. 1492). Basilica of
Santa Croce in Gerusalemme
On pages 128-129: Andrea Pozzo, *The Glory of Saint Ignatius* (1691-1694). Church of
San'Ignazio
On pages 160-161: Caravaggio, *The Calling of Saint Matthew* (1599-1600). Church of San
Luigi dei Francesi, Contarelli Chapel
On pages 172-173: View of the church of San Lorenzo in Miranda
On pages 184-185: View of the main hall of the Mosque of Rome (Paolo Portoghesi architect)

CONTENTS

HOW TO USE THIS GUIDE

THIS GUIDE introduces the reader to St. Peter's and the seven Churches of the Jubilee in Rome, the catacombs and the historic Churches. These are followed by the Churches of the world's Catholics, the "homes" of the saints, and the places of worship and other Churches and religious communities. Lastly, the Synagogue and the Mosque.

A historical
introduction illustrates the events concerning the Eternal City from the origins to the present day.

Historical facts
and an accurate historic-artistic description are provided for each Basilica.

An architectural cross-section *of the basilica illustrating the most interesting features. An introduction to the tour and all the practical information required can be found on the same page.*

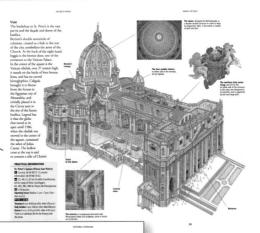

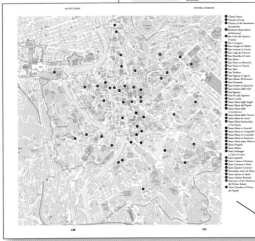

At the beginning of each chapter thematic maps *make it easy to pinpoint the Basilicas and Churches, arranged according to the best tour route.*

Accurate descriptions and practical information *are also provided for all the other Churches and places of worship of religious communities.*

THE HISTORY OF ROME

Legend has it that the basket containing the twins Romulus and Remus, the mythical founders of the city, came to rest under a fig tree. The tree was still being venerated in the Forum in Imperial times, which tells us that the early Romans' religion was animistic. The assimilation of local and foreign deities, and the introduction into Rome of the religions of conquered cities, soon transformed the original religion into an anthropomorphic and polytheistic one. Such assimilation for political

purposes was nothing new, as it was already known among other peoples, particularly in the Greek world. What was different, however, was that the Roman religion preserved all these influences, as could be seen in the exact repetition of rituals, rules and religious forms even though, as early as the Republican era, they had already lost their original spiritual meaning.

It was a pragmatic religion, whose aim was to propitiate the gods (*pax deorum*), and obtain favors for oneself or the community, in exchange for rituals often conducted by the beneficiary himself as priest (*pater familias*, magistrate, military commander). But when Eastern religions, especially mystical and orgiastic ones, were introduced in Rome, which was going through a period of great political instability at

"ROMA CAPUT MUNDI REGIT ORBIS FRENA ROTUNDI"
(Rome, capital of the world, holds the reins of the round globe.) This phrase dates back to the time of Emperor Diocletian, and it seems that it ran on his crown.

the time, its ancient political, moral and religious customs were thrown into confusion, and this brought about the collapse of the Republic. Julius Caesar was for a time the leading figure on the city's political scene, while the hope in the heart of every Roman citizen for the coming of a saviour (*mundi salvator*) who would restore peace was embodied in Octavianus, Caesar's great-nephew and adopted son, the future Augustus, who became the first Emperor (29 BC–14 AD). It was during his reign that Jesus Christ was born in Bethlehem. Octavianus adopted policies that reconciled the ancient traditions of Rome's "national" past with the need for a single leadership. He therefore accepted the title of Princeps (first among equals), and refused that of Lord, customary among Eastern rulers. The title of Augustus, bestowed on him by the Senate in 27 BC had great implications for the future. It gave him a status well above the average human being, without, however, making him a divine figure.

THE UNIVERSAL MISSION OF THE CHURCH OF ROME

Rome's Christian community encompasses many cultures, peoples and ways of thinking. Its breadth of vision creates harmony and convergence between them, as well as mutual enrichment, thus leading to unity of substance within diversity of form. It is a characteristic of Rome that all Christians can feel at home here, wherever they may come from. A sign of this richness can be found in the statistics on the Church in Rome:

- 392 male religious communities;
- 1,137 female religious communities;
- approximately 50 cardinals;
- approximately 100 bishops;
- 1,761 secular priests;
- approximately 5,000 religious priests;
- 21,500 nuns;
- 17 universities, academies and international institutes with over 1,000 professors and 7,000 students;
- 80 confraternities and archconfraternities;
- 38 associations involved in social and charitable work.

Augustus succeeded in his aim, and the Senate and the Roman people dedicated the *Ara Pacis Augustae* to him. This was a monumental altar where every year a solemn sacrifice of thanksgiving to the gods for the peace granted to the Roman world was to take place. The old religion, however, was profoundly altered by the Emperor when he proclaimed himself *Divi filius* (son of God), because Julius Caesar, his adoptive father, had been deified after his death. Augustus thus created the foundations of an Imperial cult, in which the Emperor was to be later defined as *divus* (divine) and *numen* (deity). The Emperor's deification is important to the history of the persecution of Christians, who refused to perform

The Capitoline she-wolf, in Ancient Rome a sacred animal and symbol of the city.

The Forum, the market place and later the city's political and administrative center.

sacrifices to the Emperor as god, as witnessed in the Acts and Passions of the martyrs. We know about St. Paul's first contact with Roman Christians through the letter he wrote to them in 56–57 AD, in which the Apostle communicated his intention to visit them (Romans 1:10–12). Owing to unforeseen difficulties, Paul did not arrive in Rome until the spring of the year 61 AD, and not as a free man, but as a prisoner. As he landed in Italy, at Pozzuoli near Naples, he was greeted by other believers who were living there (Acts 28:14). Pozzuoli was one of the secondary ports where the routes from the East to Rome ended. The presence of Christians there shows that missionary activity had followed the trade routes. Peter arrived in Rome soon after the date of St. Paul's letter to the Romans, but nothing is known about the two

Apostles' time together in the city. What we do know is that they were both there in 64 AD, when a great fire, which had broken out in the vicinity of the Circus Maximus, spread throughout most of the city. The Emperor Nero was held responsible for it and he in turn blamed it on the Christians, and after summary trials they were put to death in the summer of 64 AD (Tacitus, *Annals*, 15, 44). Peter was crucified and buried in the Vatican area, near other graves. Paul, as a Roman citizen, was beheaded near Tre Fontane, on the Via Ostiensis. From that moment on, a special decree banned the practice of Christianity, making even the use of the *nomen* (term) Christian a *crimen* (crime) (Tertullian, *Ad Nat.* 1, 3). The persecution of Christians spread throughout the Empire, lasting

ROME: FROM MONARCHY TO REPUBLIC				
616 Etruscan supremacy	**499** Roman victory over the Latins near Lake Regillus	**367** Power shared by patricians and plebeians		**270** Reggio conquere
700–600 BC	500–400 BC	300 BC		
754-753 Rome founded	**509** Expulsion of Tarquinius Superbus	**449** Laws of the Twelve Tables	**343-341** First war against the Samnites	**272** Taranto conquered

Christianity intensified after 324 A.D., the year that Licinius Augustus, Constantine's brother-in-law and ruler of the Eastern empire, who had started to oppress Christians once more, was defeated, and the absolute monarchy was restored.

In the beginning, it was the Apostles as a group who led the Christian community, but later on local jurisdictions were formed. During the Apostles' lifetime, two hierarchies existed: one made up of the Apostles, and the other of those whom the Apostles had appointed to head the individual communities.

The primacy of Peter, with its seat in Rome, is an institution of divine law. The office of Peter and his successors includes the role of being a sign of unity among all Churches.

The history of the Western Church is

three hundred years, which were called "the age of the persecutions" (ten, according to tradition, by analogy with the ten plagues of Egypt), or the age of the martyrs.

In 313 AD, Emperor Constantine officially recognized Christianity, thus freeing it from its centuries-long oppression. This was the beginning of an alliance that led the Church from its status of *religio illicita* (outlawed religion) to that of Imperial Catholic Church. While the new religion received preferential treatment, the old one was increasingly driven out into the rural areas; hence the word "paganism," meaning the religion of the *pagi* (country districts). The Empire's conversion to

240-237 Sicily and Sardinia conquered	**216** Roman defeat at Cannae	**146** Rome occupies Greece	**129** Conquest of the East
200 BC		**100 BC**	
266-65 The Piceno region subjugated	**217** Roman defeat on Lake Trasimene	**202** Definitive victory over the Carthaginans	**133** Spain conquered

Octavianus Augustus, Julius Caesar's heir, devoted himself to political reorganization by holding all the power himself. His policies insured a period of prosperity in Rome.

The Ara Pacis (Altar of Peace), a monument of great artistic value, was dedicated to Augustus by the Senate in 9 BC, as a sign of gratitude for the peace achieved through victorious campaigns in Spain and Gaul.

THE ROMAN SYNOD

In 382 AD the Holy Roman Church was declared first among all Churches. This decision did not stem from a Council edict nor did it come from an imperial law; it received its primacy from the words of our Lord and Saviour: "You are Peter, and on this rock I will build my church" (Matthew 16:18).

failed to maintain their identity. Nonetheless, St. Augustine had warned that, as long as the Romans remained faithful to themselves (*Sermones ad populum*), Rome would never be lost. After the sack of Rome by Alaric in 410 AD, Augustine identified in the City of God the legacy of Imperial Rome. Some years later Pope Leo the Great, who put a stop to Attila's march on Rome in 452 AD, in his famous speech *In natale Apostolorum*, proclaimed in prophetic words that wars had made Rome *caput mundi* (capital of the world) and that peace would make it *civitas sacerdotalis et regia* (a sacerdotal and royal city). His words meant that having been founded a second time by the Apostles Peter and Paul, the city was about to enter a new cycle in its history, one that would be truly catholic, i.e. universal, with its martyrs as protectors. In the Middle Ages the fact that Rome was the place of the martyrdom of Peter and Paul was of fundamental importance, and basilicas were built over their respective tombs. During Constantine's reign, the burial places of the two Apostles and of the other martyrs became centers of worship and pilgrimage. Basilicas were built above them, or close by, stairs and paths were built to provide access to the catacombs, the most venerated

also marked by barbarian invasions, which threatened the very survival of Rome, not just as a city (*urbs*) made up of buildings, monuments and streets, but also as a civil and cultural institution, if its citizens

St. Paul, the son of a Jew from the tribe of Benjamin, was a victim of the persecutions against Christians. In the photo: Michelangelo's *St. Paul* (1503–1504).

crypts were decorated, and calendars were compiled recording the names of the saints.

Excavations carried out between 1940 and 1949 revealed that Constantine had ordered that the basilica of St. Peter's be built with its high altar directly above St. Peter's tomb. This is proof that the choice of the location of sacred monuments was neither random, nor dictated by the environment, but instead closely related to the event commemorated there. Roman sanctuaries are places where memory is still alive: some have remained almost untouched, while others have been turned into basilicas. The special interest of the faithful for these places, especially the ones where the bodies of the saints were preserved, was linked to the expectation of miracles and healing being performed by the servants of Christ. Physical contact was sought in order to obtain the benefit of the healing power emanating from those holy bodies. This practice has its Gospel parallel in the episode of the woman suffering from hemorrhages: "If I only touch his cloak, I will be made well" (Matthew 9:21 and Mark 5:28); "She came up behind him and touched the fringe of his clothes, and immediately her bleeding stopped" (Luke 8:44). But Rome is not just the place that brings to mind so many witnesses of the faith: it is also the seat of Peter, who was given the keys of the kingdom of heaven (Matthew 16:19), and of his successors. This is the reason for the pilgrimage *ad limina apostolorum* (to the doors of the Apostles) and to the *cathedra Petri* (the Chair of Peter). The practice of going on a pilgrimage *ad limina apostolorum*, which also involved a donation of money (St. Peter's pence) was given a stimulus by the missionary activities of Augustine, Abbot of Sant'Andrea al Celio, and his forty fellow monks among the Anglo-Saxons who had settled in Britain.

"GO TO ROME, WHERE THE SQUARES ARE PAVED WITH GOLD"

"Jesus, the Shepherd of Shepherds, taught me the true doctrine and sent me to Rome to behold the supreme majesty and to see a queen attired in gold. There I saw a people who wear a shining seal" (from a monument carved at the end of the 2nd century AD by Abercius, Bishop of Hierapolis in Asia Minor, and now in the Vatican Museums).

"Go to Rome, where the squares are paved with gold, and stained red with the blood of the saints: there, through the indulgences obtained from the Supreme Pontiffs, thanks to their prayers, you shall find the shortest way to Heaven" (St. Bridget of Sweden, *Acta et processus*).

Caravaggio's *Crucifixion of St. Peter* (1601–1602) dramatically portrays the moment when the Apostle was crucified head down.

ORDINARY JUBILEES

1300 Boniface VIII
1350 Clement VI
1390 Urban VI
1400 Boniface IX
1423 Martin V
1450 Nicholas V
1475 Sixtus IV
1500 Alexander VI
1525 Clement VII
1550 Julius III
1575 Gregory XIII
1600 Clement VIII
1625 Urban VIII
1650 Innocent X
1675 Clement X
1700 Innocent XII - Clement XI
1725 Benedict XIII
1750 Benedict XIV
1775 Clement XIV - Pius VI
1825 Leo XII
1875 Pius IX
1900 Leo XIII
1925 Pius XI
1950 Pius XII
1975 Paul VI
2000 John Paul II

*Owing to adverse political events, the Jubilees of 1800 (Pius VI and Pius VII) and 1850 (Pius IX) were never celebrated; the 1875 Jubilee was celebrated but without ceremony.

EXTRAORDINARY JUBILEES

The first of these was declared by Leo X in 1518, to help Poland in its war against the Turks.
The number is uncertain: the 1,900th and 1,950th anniversaries of the Redemption in 1933 (Pius XI) and 1983 (John Paul II) are well known.

The number of pilgrimages increased after the Germanic peoples were converted by St. Boniface, the most important missionary in Germany, who had been sent there by Pope Gregory II in 719.

After converting the pagans, Boniface devoted himself to purifying and strengthening Christian life. He was convinced that the necessary condition for the growth of a local Church was the maintenance of close links with Rome. For this reason, in 743 he made all the Bishops gathered together for the first Council of the Eastern Franks pronounce an oath of allegiance to the Pope. The alliance of the Popes with the Franks (the Holy Roman Empire) and the split with Byzantium completed the task: Rome was reinstated as the capital of the world. From the 9th century onwards, a new system of penance was established; in this new system the appropriate penance for many sins committed over a period of time included a pilgrimage of atonement before full absolution could be obtained. Rome became the favorite destination of these penitential pilgrimages, and monasteries and hospitals were built along the routes for the welfare of pilgrims and the sick. Pilgrimages to Rome increased

This sarcophagus, currently housed in the Museo Nazionale Romano in Rome, depicts the subjugation of the barbarians by the Romans.

14

Initially the tombs and relics of the Apostles Peter and Paul were the only two reference points for Jubilee pilgrimages. Later, in 1350, Pope Urban VI added the basilica of San Giovanni in Laterano, which is the cathedral of Rome, and in 1390, on the occasion of the Holy Year, Pope Boniface IX extended the duty to include Santa Maria Maggiore, the first sanctuary dedicated to the Virgin Mary in Western Christendom. These became the "patriarchal basilicas" where, from the 1500 Jubilee onwards, simultaneous ceremonies were conducted by proxies while the Pope officiated in St. Peter's. Later, in the last quarter of the 16th century, the practice, initiated by St. Philip Neri, of visiting the seven basilicas took root: St. Peter's, San Paolo, Santa Maria Maggiore, San Giovanni in Laterano, Santa Croce in Gerusalemme, San Lorenzo and San Sebastiano. For Romans, the visit to the four major basilicas had to last thirty days,

THE CATHEDRA

The *cathedra Petri* (Chair of Peter), preserved in St. Peter's, is an oak chair decorated with strips of ivory and twelve panels depicting the labors of Hercules and six monstruous beasts. The ivory panels illustrating the stories of Hercules are probably dated to the time of Emperor Charles the Bald (875–877). Carved in classical style, they were set in the Emperor's throne, which was later donated to the Pope by the Emperor himself.

considerably during the Jubilee of 1300, proclaimed by Pope Boniface VIII, reflecting a spontaneous and genuine popular spiritual impulse at a time when it was impossible to reach the Holy Land. Pope Boniface VIII decided that the Jubilee should be celebrated only once every 100 years; Pope Benedict XII reduced the time to 50 years, until Pope Paul II (1464–1471) established that celebrations should take place every 25 years.

The cathedra Petri (Chair of Peter), preserved in St. Peter's.

Fragment of a fresco by Giotto which shows Pope Boniface VIII proclaiming the first Jubilee in 1300 (San Giovanni in Laterano).

whether or not consecutive, while for people from outside Rome it had to last fifteen days, whether or not consecutive. In 1900, Pope Leo XIII reduced this duty to twenty and ten days respectively. Eventually, in the 1933 Jubilee, Pope Pius XI reduced the visits to three, for both Roman and non-Roman visitors, with the possibility of completing them in the same day.

On the occasion of the Holy Year of 1950, Pope Pius XII prescribed one visit only for each basilica, with no time requirement. The celebration of the indulgences also required sincere repentance for one's sins through the sacrament of confession, while the recitation of the penitential Psalms, the *Pater Noster* (the Our Father) and the Creed was recommended.

The formalities of this ritual were established on the occasion of the Jubilee on December 24, 1499, at the same time as the Vatican basilica was granted definitive primacy over the cathedral of San Giovanni in Laterano, and consists of knocking down the wall of the Holy Door. This is a reminder of the Door of Justice in Jerusalem, the celestial city which the pilgrim can ideally enter on the

strength of the great pardon. It also refers to Peter, guardian of the gates of Heaven and defender against the doors of Hell that, through him, will not prevail against it (Matthew 16:18–19). At the same time, the Pope's ritual gesture of hitting the wall with a hammer repeats the gesture of Moses when he made water spring from rock in order to quench the thirst of his people. This is a divine manifestation of the source of life, and an allusion to the purifying water of Baptism.

The Jubilee is an act of penance and forgiveness that has made Rome the place of spiritual rebirth and the true center of the Christian world. From this stems the commitment of the Popes, starting from Martin V (the Roman Otto Colonna, 1417–1431), to alter the physical appearance of Rome, transforming it from City of the Sun, Heliopolis of the West, to Star of the Sea: the star shape is

THE FIRST JUBILEE

Declared in the Papal Bull *Antiquorum habet* (February 22, 1300), did not have a theological justification, unlike the Jubilee of 1350, declared by Pope Benedict XII in his Bull *Unigenitus Dei Filius* (January 27, 1343). Benedict XII's letter made official the doctrine developed by theologians on the theme of the "wealth of rewards" (*thesaurus meritorum*) at the Church's disposal, and on the communion of the saints (*communio Sanctorum*).

The walled-up Holy Door (Porta Santa) in St. Peter's, in an oil painting by the Danish artist C.W. Eckersberg (1816).

outlined by the five streets around Santa Maria Maggiore (an allusion to Mary, Star of the Sea), which in turn are joined to the cross formed by two streets (Via Pia and Via Felice).

The star shape also represents *Roma Sancta* (Holy Rome), the center from which the missionary work of the Church and Jesus Christ spreads out into the world, with Peter and Paul as its pillars.

After the Jubilee of 1450, Pope Nicholas V dreamed of creating an "ideal" Christian Rome, where newly arrived pilgrims would be able to see wonder after wonder.

The 16th-century Popes embarked on an extraordinary urban planning project, aimed at making Rome the new Jerusalem. From Alexander VI to Julius II, from Leo X to Paul III, from Pius IV to Gregory XIII, the Popes in

succession focused on the city's renewal. Sixtus V (1585–1590), a brilliant religious figure and statesman, made Rome the first modern city in Europe, giving it the appearance that marks both the culmination of Renaissance urban planning, and the birth of the Baroque city.

During the Renaissance, the Popes completely changed Rome's urban fabric, transforming it from City of the Sun to Star of the Sea, clearly an allusion to the Virgin Mary, Star of the Sea. In the photo: *Map of Rome* by I. Danti (1536).

The Seven Basilicas of Rome, an engraving attributed to Pietro de' Nobili (1575).

17

ST. PETER'S, THE SEVEN CHURCHES OF THE JUBILEE AND THE CATACOMBS

Saint Peter's in Vatican

San Paolo fuori le Mura

San Giovanni in Laterano

Santa Maria Maggiore

Santa Croce in Gerusalemme

San Lorenzo fuori le Mura

Catacombs or Sanctuaries of the Martyrs

Santa Pudenziana

San Clemente

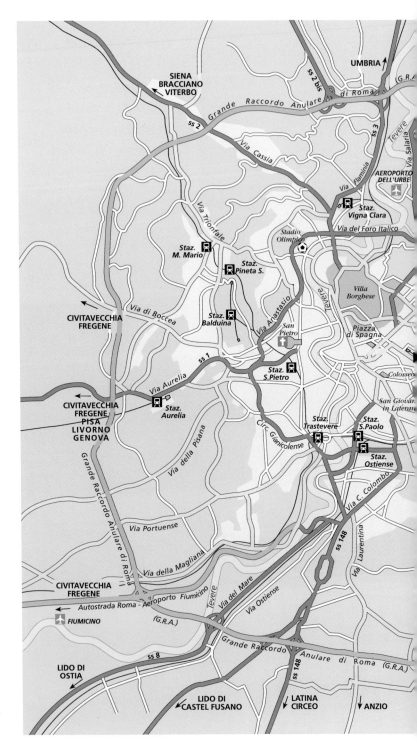

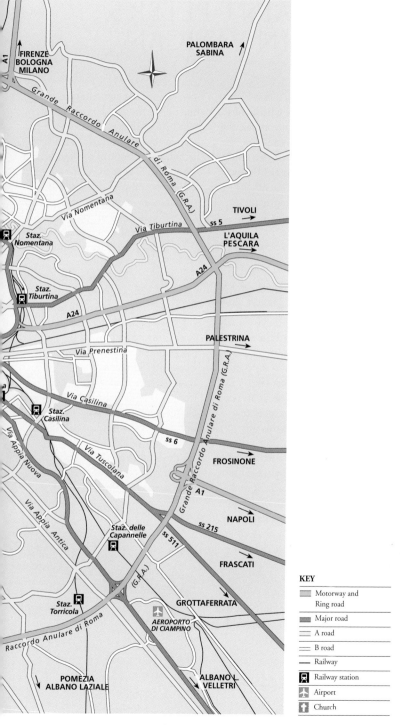

SAINT PETER'S
IN VATICAN

The Basilica of St. Peter's (San Pietro) is the spiritual center of Christianity. It is venerated because it contains the Apostle's tomb, and it symbolizes the legitimization of the Christian religion by the authority of Imperial Rome. Since 1377 it has been the official residence of the Pope, replacing San Giovanni in Laterano. During the latter half of the 2nd century, a shrine was erected in a burial ground above the Apostle's grave, next to the place where his martyrdom occurred. The historian Eusebius of Caesarea refers to it, quoting a passage by Gaius, as the "trophy," the symbol of the Apostle's victorious faith. Located in front of it was an area of 5 meters by 7, to keep devotees at a respectful distance, and this was surrounded by a red-painted wall, which soon became covered with the graffiti scratched on it by the faithful and by pilgrims as mementos of their visit to the humble tomb of the saint. A portion of this small funerary monument, including a small column, is still visible in the space called the *Confessio*, under Bernini's majestic canopy. The Emperor Constantine suggested to Pope Sylvester I (314–335) that a huge basilica be built with the Apostle's tomb as its center: this would make it a monument to

martyrdom, but also a funerary function, as it would be used as a cemetery by the faithful. In order to keep to the contours of the land, including the slope of the Vatican hill, the architects were forced to resolve some very complex problems. In addition, an open cemetery, where Christians and pagans had for centuries been buried side by side, was ordered to be closed.

This was a very serious measure, as Roman law protected all graves and cemeteries, and could only be authorized by the Emperor as Pontifex Maximus (Supreme Pontiff), which allowed him, in exceptional circumstances, to make decisions of this kind. The choice of location for the basilica is further proof, if proof were needed, of the

Depicted on the Papal coat of arms, besides the triple crown (the tiara), are the keys to the Kingdom of Heaven, given to Peter by Jesus.

The façade of St. Peter's in a print of circa 1620.

actual presence there of Peter's tomb: had it not been for the need to respect the exact location of the tomb, Constantine's engineers would no doubt have chosen a site more suitable than the slopes of a hill occupied by a cemetery and plagued by the infiltration of groundwater.

Between 319 and 324, part of the hill was made leve, thus creating a flat area measuring 290 by 90 meters, on which the foundations of the new basilica were laid. Construction must have been at an advanced stage by the time Constantine died in 337 (the building was possibly completed in 349), but little remains of it nowadays,

SAINT PETER'S IN NUMBERS

The Basilica of St. Peter's is the largest church in the world. Its floor area is 21,477 square meters, and its external perimeter is 1,778 metres. It is 186.35 meters long and 97.50 metres wide at the transept. The central nave is 46 meters high, and the dome 132.5. It contains 44 altars (compared with 120 in Constantine's basilica, of which 27 were dedicated to the Virgin Mary), 11 domes, 778 columns, 395 statues, 135 mosaic panels. A total of 99 oil lamps burn day and night around St. Peter's tomb. Bernini's canopy is the largest bronze monument in the world: it took nine years to build (1624–1633), and its columns weigh 37,000 kilos.

and we can only reconstruct its general appearance on the basis of engravings and descriptions that pre-date its rebuilding in Renaissance times.

It was a building of vast dimensions; at its front there would originally have been a narthex (a vestibule reserved for penitents), and later, under Pope Siricius (468–483), a wide four-sided loggia, with a central fountain for ritual ablutions.

Columns divided its interior into five naves, and a

more monumental tombs were erected next to the main core of the building. According to descriptions in the early sources, the basilica glowed with precious ornaments. Under St. Leo the Great (440–461), the façade was decorated with mosaics, and the central nave with a two-tiered fresco, depicting stories from the Old Testament on the right, the New Testament on the left. On the left side of the church stood the rotunda of St. Andrew whose restoration was ordered by Pope Symmachus (498–514), the Pope who built the votive chapels dedicated to St. John the Evangelist, St. John the Baptist and the Holy Cross. Nearby stood the mausoleum of the Emperor Honorius, which in the second half of the 8th century became the Church of Santa Petronilla, Royal Chapel of the Frankish kings. The magnificent tomb of the Anici was later erected behind the apse. St. Gregory the Great (590–604) transformed the area of the sanctuary, raising it by roughly one and a half meters, in order to make it possible to build the first ever semicircular crypt. This allowed the faithful to descend to approach the venerated tomb, and then leave by another staircase. The high altar was moved to the *Confessio*, the spot exactly above Peter's tomb. To the right of the façade, Pope John VII (705–707) built an oratory dedicated

transept in front of the sanctuary gave it the characteristic plan of a Latin cross, later to be used in many other basilicas.

Constantine ordered a structure covered with precious marble to be built over the Apostle's grave. Wide windows made the chamber bright, and in its floor space there was room for the tombs of the many faithful who wished to be laid to rest near the Prince of the Apostles. Later, other,

CHRONOLOGY

64 o 67 Peter buried	**1452** Nicholas V plans the restoration	**1506** Julius II lays the first stone	**1547** Michelangelo becomes the architect of St. Peter's	**1593** Completion of the dome	**1626** Consecration of the new basilica
324 Constantine builds the basilica					

AD 60–800	1500	1550	1600

Before 200 Construction of the shrine over the tomb of Peter	**1503** Julius II appoints Bramante architect of the basilica	**1538** Direction of the work assigned to Antonio da Sangallo the younger	**1606** Carlo Maderno extends the basilica	
800 Charlemagne crowned in St. Peter's		**1514** Raphael directs the work	**1564** Death of Michelangelo	**1614** Maderno completes the façade

to the Virgin Mary, demolished by Maderno at the beginning of the 17th century. Its wall decorations, depicting events in the life of Christ and the Apostles, were partially detached, and divided into panels. These found their way to various places such as the sacristy of Santa Maria in Cosmedin in Rome, in other Italian cities, and Russia.

Because of raids by the Saracens, Pope Leo IV (847–855) built a massive wall all around the "borgo di San Pietro," which was therefore known as "The Leonine City." During the first decades of the 12th century, under Pope Calixtus II (1119–1124), additional work was carried out in the

sanctuary, raising it further, in order to safeguard and preserve respect for the venerated place where Peter had been laid to rest. Another important phase occurred under Pope Innocent III (1198–1216), when a new mosaic was laid in the apse, to replace the early Christian one. It depicted Christ between Peter and Paul with, below, twelve lambs symbolizing the Apostles, and the Mystic Lamb

HISTORY OF THE BASILICA

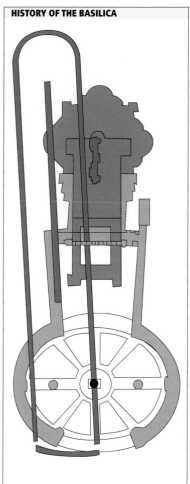

AREAS

- CIRCUS OF NERO
- CONSTANTINE
- RENAISSANCE
- BAROQUE

St. Peter was buried in 64 AD in a cemetery near the place of his crucifixion, in the Circus of Nero. Constantine started building a basilica over this spot in 324. It was demolished in the 15th century, and rebuilt in the 16th and 17th centuries. The façade was completed in 1614, and the church was consecrated in 1626.

The ancient and most venerated statue of St. Peter. Previously in the so-called "della Bocciata" Chapel, it is now at the exit of the Grottos.

Sylvester I succeeded Melchiades as Bishop in 314, and it was to him that the Emperor Constantine proposed the construction of the huge basilica of St. Peter's.

Palace. Under Pope Gregory IX (1227–1241), the decoration of the façade was renewed, and Pope Nicholas III Orsini (1277–1280) built his family chapel, and possibly commissioned the frescoes in the atrium, of which only a few fragments remain.

During the period of the exile of the Popes in Avignon, Cardinal Stefaneschi instructed Giotto to make the famous "Navicella" mosaic of Christ walking on the water and the Stefaneschi triptych for the high altar. The latter is now in the Vatican Pinacoteca, while the only remnants of the former are two angels (one in St. Peter's, the other in the town of Boville Ernica, in the province of Frosinone), and the panel was completely reworked in the 17th century.

alongside the Pope himself and the Church personified.

These last two figures, with a phoenix on a palm in the background, were detached from the wall, and are now in the Museo di Roma in the Braschi

The Basilica of Notre Dame de la Paix in Yamoussoukro, Côte d'Ivoire, is modeled after St. Peter's.

Aerial view of Saint Peter's Square.

by Charles VIII's ambassador for the Chapel of Santa Petronilla, or of the Frankish kings. The old early Christian building was in a somewhat poor state, however, and as early as during the papacy of Nicholas V, on the advice of Leon Battista Alberti, Bernardo Rossellino was asked to draw up a plan for rebuilding it. The building was to be in the form of a Latin cross, with a central dome. Work began, but in 1455 it was suspended for nearly fifty years, with the exception of a brief burst of activity under Pope Paul II. Rossellino's was the first of a long series of contributions by some of the most prominent artists of the time. An important step forward was made by Julius II (1503–1513), when he commissioned Donato Bramante, whom he chose over Giuliano da Sangallo, to direct the work, more than

Martin V (1417–1431) later restored the loggia, and Eugenius IV (1431–1447) commissioned Filarete with the task of sculpting the bronze door that was to be the main entrance to the basilica. The work was completed in 1445. Many more sculptures date from this time, although several have been lost. Others, such as the tabernacle by Donatello (1432), preserved in the Treasury of St. Peter's, have been moved. Also in the Treasury is the tomb of Sixtus IV (1471–1484) by Antonio di Jacopo Benci, known as Antonio del Pollaiolo, while the memorial to Innocent VIII (1484–1492) can still be seen inside the basilica.

The last years of the 15th century saw the completion of Michelangelo's masterpiece, the *Pietà*, commissioned

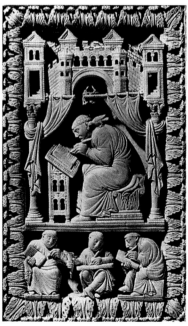

Light pours in on Bernini's wooden "Chair of St. Peter" in the apse from a wide window at the center of which shines a dove, representing the Holy Ghost.

St. Gregory the Great at his writing desk, an ivory panel from the 10th century. As Pope, between 590 and 604, he made important decisions regarding the renovation of the basilica.

work went ahead under Vignola, followed in 1573 by Giacomo della Porta, and the dome was eventually inaugurated in 1593.

Many other important features of the basilica, including the façade, were still unfinished. Carlo Maderno carried out the work, completing it between 1606 and 1614 with the addition of three new chapels on each side of the nave. Maderno's contribution considerably altered the sobriety of the original designs by Bramante and Michelangelo, in which the interior walls were to be simply plastered, not richly adorned with colored marble and other ornaments.

A chapel in honor of Gregory XIII (1572–1585) was built in the space beneath one of the smaller domes, and there was a plan for the central dome to be decorated with mosaics for the Jubilee of 1600, but work on it was completed after the event.

In 1624, on the orders of Pope Urban VIII, Bernini started working on his gilded bronze canopy, with its massive spiral columns. It was officially

a century after its conception. This plan was for a Greek-cross building, with a large central dome, and four small secondary domes. After Bramante's death in 1511, the task was taken up by Raphael, Fra Giocondo da Verona, and Antonio da Sangallo. The Greek-cross plan was again changed to one based on a Latin cross, with a lengthened aisle and a raised floor, in order to create the space for the Vatican Grottos beneath it.

After Sangallo's death in 1546, Michelangelo took over responsibility for the project, and attempted to return to Bramante's original design. The impact of his work can still be seen, especially in the area around the apse of the new basilica. He died before the dome was completed. The

ARNOLFO DI CAMBIO

Commissioned by Boniface VIII, he took part in the building of the votive chapel dedicated to Boniface IV, and placed, with its octagonal dome, against the inner wall of the façade. Boniface IV is portrayed inside his sarcophagus, as well as in a roundel by Jacopo Torriti, which shows Peter and Paul presenting him to the Virgin and the Child. Both these works are now in the Grottos. Arnolfo di Cambio is attributed the bronze statue of St. Peter, which was originally in the oratory of San Martino, since demolished, and has now been placed next to the basilica's northeastern pier. Some scholars believe it to be early Christian, but recent research seems to have definitively ruled this out.

The bronze statue of St. Peter, attributed to Arnolfo di Cambio, housed in the basilica.

THE "VERONICA" IN ST. PETER'S

The symbolic image of the pilgrimage to Rome is Christ's portrait on a piece of cloth; hence, the name "Veronica," from *vera icona*, meaning "true icon." It has been venerated as the *Sudarium Christi* (Christ's Kerchief) during every Jubilee since 1300 by pilgrims, to whom it is exhibited on Fridays and holy days. Moreover, it is one of the three most important relics in St. Peter's; the other two are a fragment of the Cross and the spear that pierced Christ's chest. From the 12th century onwards, it was generally believed that the venerated relic was the veil with which, according to tradition, Veronica dried the sweat on Jesus' face as he climbed the slopes of Calvary. The cult of this icon was especially encouraged by Innocent III when in 1216 he saw the veil turn over in its reliquary after the customary

"Procession of the Veronica" from St. Peter's to the Ospedale di Santo Spirito. Believing this was a sign, the Pope wrote a prayer which gave an indulgence of ten days (the first instance in history of a prayer connected with an indulgence). Dante saw the relic during the Jubilee of 1300, and extols it in *Paradiso*, XXXI, 103–108, while Petrarch makes a significant reference to it in the *Canzoniere*, XVI.

consecrated by the Pope in 1626, although it was not completed until 1633. In 1629 Bernini was appointed architect of St. Peter's, and continued to work there for about half a century. He designed the interior decoration, which acquired the rich ornamentation and vivid coloring of Baroque, as well as the memorials to Urban VIII and Alexander VII, the throne in the apse and the famous colonnade.

View of St. Peter's Square thronged with the faithful.

The "Veronica" with Sts. Peter and Paul, Ugo da Carpi, Fabric of St. Peter's, the Vatican.

Visit

The backdrop to St. Peter's is the vast parvis and the façade and dome of the basilica.

Bernini's double semicircle of columns, created as a link to the rest of the city, symbolizes the arms of the Church. At the back of the right-hand loggia is the bronze door, one of the entrances to the Vatican Palace.

In the center of the square is the Vatican obelisk, over 37 meters high; it stands on the backs of four bronze lions, and has no carved hieroglyphics. Caligula brought it to Rome from the forum in the Egyptian city of Alexandria, and initially placed it in the Circus next to the site of the future basilica. Legend has it that the globe that stood at its apex until 1586, when the obelisk was moved to the center of the square, contained the ashes of Julius Caesar. The hollow cross at the top is said to contain a relic of Christ's

Bernini's canopy

Stairs to the dome

Central nave

The interior is sumptuously decorated with Renaissance inlays and sculptures, some of which are by Bernini.

PRACTICAL INFORMATION

St. Peter's Square (Piazza San Pietro)

Sacristy: 06 69 88 37 12; tourist information: 06 69 88 16 62.

23, 49, 31, 62 for Via della Conciliazione, 64 for Largo di Porta Cavalleggeri, 81, 492, 982, 990 for Piazza del Risorgimento

A Ottaviano.

Opening hours: Basilica 7 a.m.–7 p.m. (Oct.– Mar. 6 p.m.).

Treasury 8 a.m.–6:50 p.m. (Oct.–Mar. 5:30 p.m.)
Holy Grottos 7 a.m.–5:40 p.m. (Oct.–Mar. 6:40 p.m.)
Dome 8 a.m.–5:45 p.m.(Oct.–Mar. 4:45 p.m.)
There is an admission fee for the Treasury and the dome.

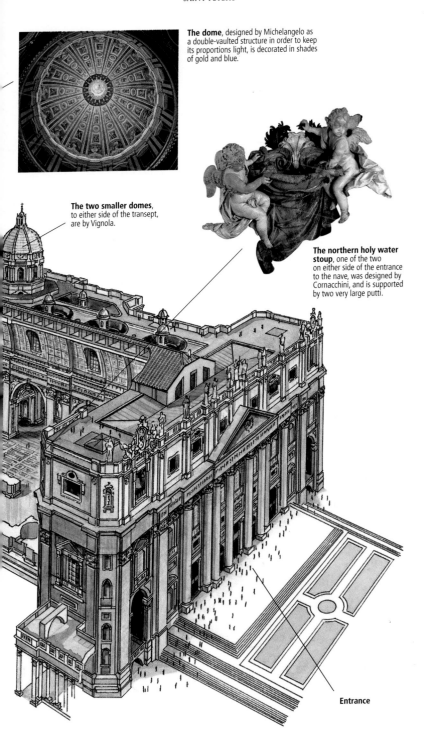

The dome, designed by Michelangelo as a double-vaulted structure in order to keep its proportions light, is decorated in shades of gold and blue.

The two smaller domes, to either side of the transept, are by Vignola.

The northern holy water stoup, one of the two on either side of the entrance to the nave, was designed by Cornacchini, and is supported by two very large putti.

Entrance

31

Cross. The paving around the obelisk is designed as a compass rose, indicating the direction of the various winds.

Between March and September 1586, while Sixtus V was Pope, Domenico Fontana used 150 horses and 47 winches to move the obelisk to its present position. The two fountains that complete the visual symmetry of the square date from the 17th century; the one on the right was designed by Carlo Maderno.

The Holy Door, walled up from the inside, is the last on the right-hand side of the atrium of St. Peter's. There are similar ones in the basilicas of San Paolo, San Giovanni in Laterano and

Santa Maria Maggiore. It symbolizes the metaphysical threshold that man has to cross in order to achieve salvation (John 10: 9), and it is never opened, except by the Pope in the solemn ceremony marking the start of the Jubilee year, both ordinary and extraordinary. In a special ritual, the Pope kneels and strikes the brick wall three times with a hammer, saying: "O Lord, allow your Church to live joyfully this auspicious moment, when you have chosen to open this door, for your faithful to enter and raise their prayers to you: this way, having obtained forgiveness, indulgence and the full remission of their sins, they will quicken their step along a life led according to the Gospel of your Son..." It is through this door, closed by the Pope himself in another ceremony to end each

On the parapet above the attic story of the façade stand thirteen large statues of Christ, St. John the Baptist and all the Apostles except St. Peter.

The bronze door by Vico Consorti as we see it today was inaugurated on December 24, 1949, to replace the wooden one carved in 1749.

THE PANELS OF THE HOLY DOOR

1	2	3	4
5	6	7	8
9	10	11	12
13	14	15	16
Epigraph A		Epigraph B	

1 The cherub at the gate of Paradise

2 The expulsion from Paradise. *Quod Heva tristis abstulit* (What unhappy Eve took away)

3 May, Our Lady of the Annunciation. *Tu reddis almo germine* (You restore through your Divine Son)

4 The Angel of the Annunciation

5 Jesus baptized in the Jordan. *Tu venis ad me?* (Are you coming to me?)

6 The lost sheep. *Salvare quod perierat* (To rescue what had been lost)

7 The merciful Father. *Pater, peccavi in coelum et coram te* (Father, I have sinned against Heaven and before you)

8 The healing of the paralytic. *Tolle garbum tuum et ambula* (Take up your bed and walk)

9 The sinful woman is forgiven. *Remittuntur ei peccata multa* (Her many sins are forgiven)

10 The duty of forgiveness. *Septuages septies* (Seventy times seven)

11 Peter's denial. *Conversus Dominus respexit Petrum* (And the Lord turned and looked at Peter)

12 Heaven given to a thief. *Hodie mecum eris in Paradiso* (Today you shall be with me in Paradise)

13 The appearance to Thomas. *Beati qui crediderunt* (Blessed are those who have believed)

14 The risen Christ appears in the upper room. *Accipite Spiritum Sanctum* (Receive the Holy Spirit)

15 The Risen Christ appears to Saul. *Sum Jesus quem tu persequeris* (I am Jesus, whom you are persecuting)

16 The opening of the Holy Door. *Sto ad ostium et pulso* (I stand at the door and knock)

Epigraph A: history of the Holy Door

Epigraph B: spiritual greetings to those who cross the threshold of the shrine

The panels of the Holy Door, executed by Vico Consorti for the Jubilee of 1950, represent, through the depiction of the episodes from the Bible, original sin, as well as the salvation and forgiveness brought to mankind from Christ. Right: Mary, Our Lady of the Annunciation. Left: The Risen Christ appears to Saul.

Holy Year, that pilgrims enter to obtain their indulgences.

Above the door there are two stone plaques, one commemorating the ordinary Jubilee of 1975, celebrated by Paul VI, and the other the extraordinary Jubilee of Redemption, proclaimed by John Paul II in 1983-1984.

The façade was created by Maderno (1607–1614) by moving the front elevation forward, and is preceded by a flight of steps designed by Bernini, which in turn is flanked by two 19th-century statues of Peter and Paul. At the two ends of the façade are two archways, the one on the left known as the "Arch of the Bells." In the center, higher up on the façade, is the Loggia of Benedictions, where the Pope appears on special occasions, and where the solemn announcement of the election of the new Pope is made.

There are two equestrian statues at the far ends of the atrium: one is of Constantine, by Bernini, the other is of Charlemagne, by Agostino Cornacchini (1725). The last opening on the right is the Holy Door, which is opened at the beginning of each Holy Year, and above it on the left is the epigraph of the Bull in which Boniface VIII proclaimed the first Jubilee in 1300. Opposite the main door is the famous mosaic of the "Navicella," a 17th-century copy of the lost original by Giotto, which used to be in the old four-sided loggia.

The present nave has the typical appearance of a church from the period of the Counter-Reformation, with its massive piers with Corinthian decorations connected by arches 13 meters high and 23 meters wide. The first three arches correspond to the extension of the front of the basilica designed by Maderno. An axis line marked on the floor shows, although not precisely, the lengths of other great basilicas of Christendom, all smaller, however, than St. Peter's. The naves and the arms of the transept are graced by 38 statues, made between the eighteenth and the twentieth centuries, of the founders of great religious orders, such as St. Teresa of Avila, St. Vincent de Paul, St. John Bosco,

---

THE INSCRIPTIONS INSIDE THE BASILICA

Along the frieze of the powerful entablature supporting the dome is a long Latin inscription in large black mosaic letters on a gold background.

On the left wall: "But I have prayed for you that your own faith may not fail; and you, when once you have turned back, strengthen your brothers" (Luke 22:32).

On the right wall: "Whatever you bind on earth will be bound in heaven, and whatever you loose on earth will be loosed in heaven" (Matthew 16:19).

On the drum of the dome "You and Peter, and on this rock I will build my church. I will give you the keys of the kingdom of heaven" (Matthew 16:18).

On the entablature of the right transept: "Simon Peter, you answered: You are the Messiah, the Son of the living God. And Jesus answered him: Blessed are you, Simon son of Jonah! For flesh and blood has not revealed this to you" (Matthew 16: 16–17).

Above the entablature of the apse, in Latin on the left-handed side, and in Greek on the right, in a shorter form: "Shepherd of the Church, feed my lambs and tend my sheep" (John 21:15).

On the entablature of the left transept: "Peter, Jesus asks you three times: Do you love me? And you, the chosen one, answer him three times: Lord, you know everything; you know that I love you" (John 21:17).

THE CORONATION OF CHARLEMAGNE
In the nave, near the entrance, there is a round porphyry slab. It was here that Charlemagne knelt to be crowned Emperor by Pope Leo III on Christmas night, 800 AD. This ritual was repeated by the 21 monarchs who came after him. In the illustration: the coronation of Charlemagne, taken from *Grandes Chroniques de France*, a 14th-century French manuscript.

St. Camillus de Lellis, St. Ignatius Loyola, St. Francis di Paola, St. Gaetano Thiene and St. Frances Xavier Cabrini. On the last pier is the bronze statue of St. Peter seated on a 19th-century marble throne, giving a blessing while holding the keys in his left hand. Recent research has confirmed that it was probably made by Arnolfo Cambio in the late 13th century. Some scholars, however, maintain that it is an early Christian sculpture, dating back to the 5th century, and moved into the basilica in the Middle Ages. The right foot of the statues shows obvious signs of wear: this is because of the tradition since the Middle Ages of pilgrims kissing it. Above it on the pier is a roundel dedicated to Pius IX, who was Pope for a very long time (32 years, 1846 to 1878), even longer than Peter. Running along the frieze of the entablature is a wall inscription on a gold background which records in Greek and Latin the words used by Jesus to found the Church. The focal point of the basilica is Bernini's bronze canopy. The four large statues, five meters high, inside the niches at the foot of the piers supporting the dome, were commissioned by Pope Urban VIII (1643); the statue of St. Longinus is by Bernini himself. Under the canopy, Maderno's *Confessio* is permanently lit by 99 lamps, burning on the site of Peter's tomb. The first chapel along the right aisle is named after the *Pietà*, the famous marble group by Michelangelo which is housed there. The work was commissioned by the Cardinal Legate of Charles VIII to Pope Alexander VI, and it is the only work signed by the great artist (his signature is visible on the sash across Mary's chest). Since it was attacked and damaged in 1971, the work is

The coronation of Charlemagne in a 14th-century French manuscript.

The canopy, with its 20-meter high spiral columns, was built by Bernini as commissioned by Urban VIII in 1624.

now protected by a thick glass pane. On the right, under the memorial to Leo XII, is the entrance to the Chapel of the Relics, containing a valuable wooden crucifix attributed to Pietro Cavallini. In the next chapel, dedicated to St. Sebastian, there are memorials to Pius XI and Pius XII, who were Popes during the 20th century, as well as the tomb of Innocent XI. The third chapel, named after the Blessed Sacrament, has a gate designed by Francesco Borromini, and a gilded bronze tabernacle by Bernini (1674) in the front of the Trinity altarpiece,

THE LARGEST CHURCHES IN THE WORLD

These lengths are engraved on the floor of the central nave of St. Peter's.

1) St. Peter's in the Vatican: 186.36 m
2) St. Paul's, London: 158.10 m
3) The Duomo in Florence: 149.28 m
4) Sacred Heart of Jesus, Brussels: 140.94 m
5) Immaculate Conception, Washington, D.C.: 139.14 m
6) Rheims Cathedral (France): 138.69 m
7) The Duomo in Milan and Cologne Cathedral: 134.94 m
8) Speyer Cathedral (Germany): 134 m
9) San Petronio, Bologna: 132.54 m
10) Seville Cathedral: 132 m
11) San Paolo fuori le Mura, Rome: 131.66 m
12) Notre Dame, Paris: 130 m
13) St. Vitus, Prague: 124 m
14) Toledo Cathedral: 122 m
15) San Giovanni in Laterano, Rome: 121.84 m
16) La Plata Cathedral (Argentina): 120 m
17) Mexico City Cathedral: 119.55 m
18) Antwerp Cathedral (Belgium): 118.60 m
19) Santa Giustina, Padua: 118.50 m
20) Esztergom Cathedral (Hungary) and Ferrara Cathedral: 118 m
21) Basilica of Santa Maria degli Angeli, Assisi: 114.76 m
22) St. Paul's, Brasilia: 111.45 m
23) Westminster Cathedral, London: 110 m
24) Hagia Sophia, Istanbul: 109.57 m
25) Cathedral of the Holy Cross, Boston: 103.50 m
26) Basilica of the Virgin Mary, Gdansk (Poland): 103.50 m
27) St. Patrick's Cathedral, New York: 101.19 m

a 17th-century work by Pietro da Cortona. Worthy of note in the Gregorian Chapel, by Giacomo della Porta (1583), is the venerated image of the Madonna of Succour, dating back to the 11th century, and already in the earlier basilica.

The right transept contains the monument to Pope Clement XIII, shown kneeling in prayer, one of the masterpieces of Antonio Canova (1784–1792). The bronze Chair of St. Peter takes center stage in the middle of the apse. It was made by Bernini (1656–1665), and it incorporates the chair, made of wood with ivory panels, that belonged to Charles the Bald in the 9th century, and later became a possession of the Popes. Known as *Cathedra Petri*, its panels depict mythological scenes from the labors of Hercules, and a king, who could be either Charles the Bald or Charlemagne. On Christmas night in the year 800, Charlemagne was crowned Emperor in St. Peter's by Pope Leo III.

The chair is supported by the large statues of the four great Doctors of the Church, and above it the dove of the Holy Spirit appears in the center of an alabaster window, in a setting of praising angels and putti. To the right of the raised area of the apse is a niche containing the monument to Urban VIII by Bernini (1627–1647), while to the left is the monument to Paul III, sculpted by Guglielmo della Porta (1551–1575).

The Chapel of the Column contains a marble altarpiece by Alessandro Algardi, depicting the meeting of St. Leo the Great with Attila (1646–1650), and a much venerated

image of the Virgin Mary.
Beyond the left transept, and separate
from the basilica, is the Sacristy; to
the right of it is a list with the names
of all the Popes buried in St. Peter's,
from the Apostle himself to John Paul I.

The mortal remains of St. Gregory
the Great, intiator of important works
in the earlier basilica, and a great
Doctor of the Church, are preserved
in the Clementine Chapel, which also
contains the tomb of Pius VII, to a

The Chapel of San Pietro, in the Vatican Grottoes,
was decorated during the papacy of Clement VIII
(1592–1638).

Michelangelo's Pietà, carved from a single block of Carrara marble in 1499, can be seen in the former Chapel of Santa Petronilla, the first in the basilica's right-hand nave.

design by the Danish Neoclassical sculptor Bertel Thorvaldsen (1823). In the left nave is the Chapel of the Choir, designed by Maderno. After that is the Chapel of the Presentation, containing the monument to John XXIII by Emilio Greco. Beyond this is the baptistery, whose font is a porphyry sarcophagus dating back to the time of Hadrian, and later used as a tomb for the Emperor Otto II.

The Vatican Grottos are located in the area beneath the central nave and also include part of the Vatican cemetery. There are several mausoleums, some with clear evidence of Christian conversion, and fragments of sculptures, walls and architectural elements belonging to the earliest place of worship. The Grottos also contain the tombs of many Popes, from St. Peter to John Paul I. Various chapels open onto the visitor's route. Among these, the one closest to Peter's tomb is the Clementine Chapel, or Chapel of San Pietro. Commissioned by Clement VIII, it is richly decorated in stucco and multicolored marble. The altar was built in place of an earlier 16th-century altar. Located in the area of the *Confessio* is the niche of the Pallii; it is important because traces of Peter's tomb as it was in the 2nd century, when a small memorial shrine was built above it, can be seen inside it. The most important excavations were carried out between 1940 and 1957, and clarified the complex topography of the area, and the various archaeological periods involved. Of special interest are the mausoleums from the Imperial Roman era, usually decorated with stucco, mosaics or frescoes. In some of them Christian iconography is clearly visible. One of these is the mausoleum of the Giulii, which contains fragments of a 3rd-century wall mosaic with pictures of Christ the Sun, the Good Shepherd, the prophet Johan and a fisherman.

SAN PAOLO FUORI LE MURA

What we see today is the reconstruction of the basilica after it was partially destroyed by fire on the night of July 15 to 16, 1823. It was further ravaged by restoration work that did not even spare the frescoes of the central nave, painted by Pietro Cavallini in the 13th century.

Having survived in its entirety until that date, the basilica has since then undergone a series of attempts to restore it to its original appearance. Conservative restoration, however, and the use, often out of context, of some parts of the building that had survived the disaster, do not sit well with the new stylistic solutions adopted in the 19th century and at the beginning of the twentieth. For this reason, the basilica can be seen as a clear example of "reconstructed authenticity."

The mortal remains of the Apostle, laid to rest in the cemetery alongside the Via Ostiense like those of any other victim of execution, immediately became the object of cult and veneration for Christians who, like Timothy, had had faith in him up to his death, and had converted to the Gospel.

Over his grave a *cella memoriae*, a kind of funeral shrine, was built, which soon began to attract pilgrims and believers. Here they found the inspiration to continue the difficult task of converting polytheistic peoples, using the method the saint had taught them: going from town to town, preaching in synagogues and founding core groups of believers with whom to maintain strong links even from a distance, by letters or other means. Because of its extraordinary power of inspiration, the Apostle's *cella memoriae* has never been removed, although it has changed somewhat over time.

The *Liber Pontificalis* states that it was the Emperor Constantine who erected a place of worship on Paul's tomb, consecrated on November 18, 324, during the papacy of Sylvester I (314–335). The apse of that building was placed in the opposite direction from the present one, at a tangent to the old line of the Via Ostiense. Originally rather modest in size, it was enlarged between 384 and 386

St. Paul suffered martyrdom by beheading: it was said that where his head fell three fountains sprang from the ground. His body was buried on the estate of the Roman matron Lucina, approximately 3 kilometres from where he was executed.

The basilica before the 1823 fire, in an engraving by G.B. Piranesi. Important archaeological finds, such as niches for storing ashes, and graves for paupers and freedmen, have confirmed the existence of a cemetery beneath and surrounding the basilica.

under the Emperors Valentinian II, Theodosius and Arcadius, who entrusted the building work to Cyriades, a *professor mechanicus*, i.e. an engineer. He built a church of five naves, with 80 columns and a four-sided portico, which, according to the inscription in its triumphal arch, was consecrated in 390 by Pope Siricius and completed in 395 under the Emperor Honorius.

In the middle of the 5th century, under St. Leo the Great, there began a long succession of restoration and improvement works, demonstrating the Church's special love for this basilica. Among other things, Leo was responsible for the restoration

ST. PAUL IN ROME

The saint arrived in Rome for the first time in 61 AD as a prisoner awaiting trial. Along the Via Appia, Christians from the capital came to meet him. Paul had been brought to Rome because Jews from Asia Minor had recognized him in the temple of Jerusalem and had tried to lynch him. He was saved by a tribune, who dragged him from the throng and arrested him. Having appealed on the grounds of his Roman citizenship, he was tried by the Imperial court in Rome, and not in Jerusalem. He spent two years in military custody in Rome, and it was during this time that he wrote his famous letters. As his accusers did not appear in court, he was acquitted, and the alleged offence was expunged. After the great fire of 64 AD, Paul was identified by Nero as the leader of a movement that was threatening the very existence of the establishment. Paul was arrested a second time, and locked up in the Tullianum, part of the Mamertine prison. He was condemned to death by beheading, probably in 67 AD, and martyred at Aquae Salviae outside the Aurelian Walls.

THE SAINT'S NAME ON THE STONE
The marble slab (4th or 5th century) bears the inscription with the saint's name. It has three openings (a round one for the incense-burner, and two irregular ones added after the inscription which illustrate the strength of popular faith among the pilgrims, since from those openings they would lower pieces of cloth (*brandea*) in order to touch the mortal remains of the saint and try and obtain relics of them.

of the mosaic decoration on the triumphal arch. Symmachus (498–514) ordered the reconstruction of the apse, by then unsafe, and the building of *habitacula* (dwellings for the poorer pilgrims), later renovated by Sergius I (687–701). Gregory the Great (590–604) ordered the floor of the transept to be raised and linked to the naves. Adrian I (772–795) was responsible for the new floor of the atrium, and Leo III (795–816) for the first use of marble in a pavement.

To Gregory II (715–731), on the other hand, is attributed the continuous presence of Benedictine monks at the Apostle's tomb; they are still there today. In order to defend a place that had already been plundered by Lombards and Saracens, John VIII (872–882) built a circle of walls and towers around it, creating a veritable citadel, later named "Johannipolis" (city of John), while the bell-tower was erected in the 11th century beside the small nave on the north side near the façade.

In the course of the 13th century the basilica was at its most magnificent. Many of the works of art that survived, intact or in part, the fire of 1823 belong to this period. Among them is the precious canopy by Arnolfo di Cambio, the ornamentation of the façade by Pietro Cavallini, the wonderful cloisters, and the Paschal candle-stick. The site was universally renowned as a treasure house of religious art, as well as an essential stopping place in the pilgrimage to Rome. Boniface IX (1389–1404) started the tradition of carrying out

CHRONOLOGY

		11th century			
18 November 324 Consecration of the place of worship built above Paul's tomb	**450** Start of a long succession of restoration works, lasting 300 years	Building of the bell-tower	**1724** The portico is rebuilt and a series of restorations are completed	**1826** The architect Belli begins the rebuilding work, funded by donations from the faithful
300	**400–1000**	**1000–1700**		**1800**
395 The basilica is completed after 11 years	**882** Completion of the circle of walls and towers ("Johannipolis")	**1220–1285** The cloisters, the ornamentation of the façade and the canopyare added	**15 July 1823** During the night the basilica is almost entirely destroyed by fire	**1840** Consecration of the new building

entrusting the task to Antonio Canevari. He demolished the ancient narthex and removed the remaining columns belonging to the four-sided early Christian portico. That same year the Chapel of the Crucifix was built, known today as the Chapel of the Blessed Sacrament, whose purpose was to house the miraculous 14th-century wooden crucifix. Many of these layers of history and centuries-old artistic and architectural treasures, gathered under one roof, went up in smoke during that terrible night in 1823; an integrated expression of art, architecture and religion was almost entirely lost. Popes, architects and Catholic intellectuals were called upon to meet the challenge of reproducing its lost authenticity: a particularly difficult challenge at a time which, following

restorations and improvements to coincide with Jubilees, by giving generous indulgences connected with the restoration of the basilica. Martin V reinforced this tradition in his Bull of September 4, 1423, when he asked the faithful to give donations for the restoration of the church and the monastery attached to it. Later, Gregory XIII used the occasion of the 1575 Jubilee to commission paintings to decorate the area of the sanctuary, and a balustrade to surround the Apostle's tomb. In 1600, during the papacy of Clement VIII, the high altar was erected. A newly built portico collapsed a year before the 1725 Jubilee, and Benedict XIII ordered its immediate reconstruction,

Pope Honorius III ratifies the Rule of the Dominican Order in 1216 (detail from a painting by Leandro Bassano, Venice, Church of Santi Giovanni e Paolo).

The Coronation of Boniface IX, detail from the *Chronicles of Froissart*, a 15th-century manuscript.

the age of Enlightenment, was dominated by secular ideas. Figures from the field of culture, literature and politics urged Leo XII to start rebuilding the basilica. So, on January 25, 1825, the Pope sent all the bishops the letter *Ad plurimas easque gravissimas*, asking them to start collecting donations from the faithful, in order to set in motion what was to be the largest church building project in the whole of the 19th century. Believers from all over the world responded to the appeal; while many sent money, the Viceroy of Egypt donated alabaster columns, and Tsar Nicholas I sent blocks of malachite, which were used for the two side altars in the transept. Work started in September 1826, with Belli as architect, following Valadier's preliminary plan: the Arch

of Galla Placidia was demolished and the four-sided portico was reinstated. On October 5, 1840, Pope Gregory XVI solemnly consecrated the altar of the *Confessio*, with its restored canopy above.

THE STRUCTURE OF THE BASILICA

On the inside the basilica is 131.66 meters long, 65 meters wide and 29.70 meters high. It has 80 monolithic columns made of granite from Montórfano, which divide it into five naves, the central one of which is 24.60 meters wide.

The four-sided portico, built by Guglielmo Calderini in 1928, is 70 meters long. The front features 10 monolithic columns, 10 meters high, made of pink granite from Baveno; on each side is a double row of columns, and on the side facing the Tiber a triple row, for a total of 146 columns.

High up inside there are 36 frescoes depicting events in the saint's life with, underneath, a frieze containing the portraits of all 265 Popes, from Peter to Benedict XVI.

The interior of the basilica in 1823 after the fire, in an engraving by Luigi Rossini.

The façade of San Paolo fuori le Mura.

Visit

On entering from the west through a wrought-iron gate, one is immediately struck by the solemn and majestic statue of St. Paul, carved in Carrara marble by Giuseppe Obici (1817–1878), and by the vast four-sided portico opposite the façade, built by Guglielmo Calderini between 1890 and 1928 to the original design by Luigi Poletti. An *atrium* enclosed by a portico existed in front of the basilica in ancient times, but Calderini's building, partly because it is so much larger, bears no resemblance to it. The idea of the four sides, each 70 meters long, came from the belief that they were essential to the reconstruction of a true early Christian basilica. Both the north and south sides have solid walls covered in travertine marble; the principal frontage has three rows of imposing columns, the north and south sides have two, and the narthex one. The side walls are decorated with medallions representing the symbols of the Evangelists, portraits of St. Paul's disciples, and symbols of early Christian worship. The upper part of the façade is

The Statue of St. Benedict in the chapel of the same name in the right-hand transept. Members of the oldest monastic order, Benedictines have officiated in the basilica for centuries.

The mosaic of the triumphal arch

The Gregorian porch

PRACTICAL INFORMATION

Via Ostiense, 186.

📞 06 541 03 41.

🚌 23, 128, 170, 670, 707, 761, 769.

Ⓜ Basilica di San Paolo.

Opening hours: 7:30 a.m.–6:30 p.m.; cloister: 9 a.m.–6 p.m.

The Arch of Galla Placidia: a mistaken interpretation of the two verses written on its edge has led to the belief that the arch was commissioned by the Emperor Honorius, brother of Galla Placidia.

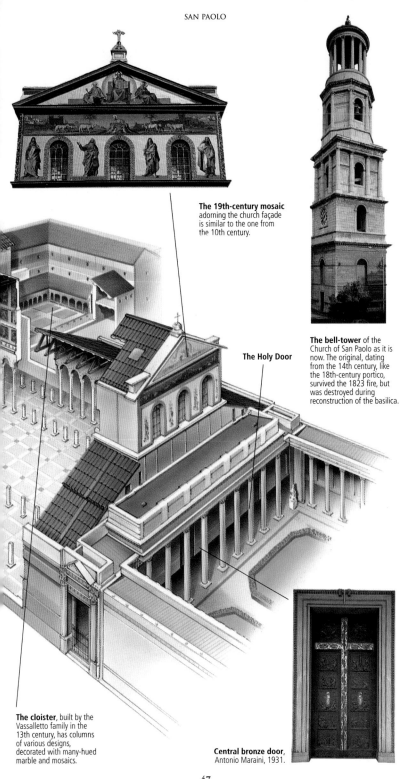

The 19th-century mosaic adorning the church façade is similar to the one from the 10th century.

The bell-tower of the Church of San Paolo as it is now. The original, dating from the 14th century, like the 18th-century portico, survived the 1823 fire, but was destroyed during reconstruction of the basilica.

The Holy Door

The cloister, built by the Vassalletto family in the 13th century, has columns of various designs, decorated with many-hued marble and mosaics.

Central bronze door, Antonio Maraini, 1931.

47

decorated with mosaics based on designs by Filippo Agricola (1795–1857) and Nicola Consoni (1814–1884), and completed between 1854 and 1874. The lower section, between the windows, shows the prophets of the Old Testament: Isaiah, Jeremiah, Ezekiel and Daniel. The middle section shows the Lamb of God on the mountain of Paradise, with four rivers, symbolizing the Gospels, flowing from it, and twelve lambs (the Apostles) drinking from them. They appear separate from Jerusalem and Bethlehem, the holy cities that here provide only the geographical and allegorical context for the biblical interpretation. Higher up, on the pediment, Christ is depicted with his hand raised in blessing between Peter and Paul, and above is the Cross, eternally central to Christian experience.

Three doors can be seen in the bottom part of the façade: the middle one is the imposing double bronze door sculpted by Antonio Maraini in 1931. Its iconography was inspired by the work of Blessed Ildefonso Schuster, Abbot of San Paolo and later Archbishop of Milan.

The entrance to the basilica, through the wrought-iron gate. In the center is the statue of St. Paul, carved in Carrara marble by Giuseppe Obici.

The door is 7.48 meters high and 3.35 meters wide, and it depicts episodes in the lives of Peter and Paul, with embossed silver vine shoots in the shape of the cross. The interior of the church gives one the impression of a very vast space: this is due to its size, the four rows of 20 monolithic granite columns supporting round arches, the absence of side chapels, and its marble pavement. All these combine to create an imposing space, where 19th-century faith attempts to interpret the original Christian experience. The Byzantine door, installed in 1967 to close off the Holy Door, was, before the fire, the main entrance to the basilica (having the same function as Maraini's bronze door). It still shows the aesthetic refinement of the 11th century in its two halves, each divided into six vertical bands of 54 panels. The panels depict scenes from the life of Christ and the Apostles, in addition to two eagles and two crosses. From the middle of this vast space, one can see the series of portraits of all the Popes, down to John Paul II. Begun by Pius IX in 1847, they are crafted in mosaic, and are the object of study in theological colleges, as evidence of the true succession of Popes. This series is a unique feature of the patriarchal basilica, setting it apart from all other

THE INTERIOR
The imposing central nave lined by 40 columns. The interior of the basilica, in the form of a Latin cross, was initiated by Pasquale Belli, but completed by Luigi Poletti, master of works from 1833 to 1869. Along the walls, the arched windows have panes made of extremely thin sheets of alabaster, a gift from King Fuad I of Egypt. At the far end are the apse and the triumphal arch, the latter also called the Arch of Galla Placidia, after the sister of Emperor Honorius, who paid for it to be built.

Detail of the bronze door at the main entrance to the basilica, by Antonio Maraini (1931), has panels decorated with bas-relief and silver.

The central nave of the Church of San Paolo.

churches in the world.
Above the medallions, along the upper section of the walls of the central nave and transept, the space between the windows is painted with 36 frescoes depicting episodes from the life of Paul, taken from the Acts of the Apostles. With the help of private sponsorship, Pius IX initiated the project, entrusting it to 22 artists, who completed it in 1860, after only three years. It is judged stylistically successful as a unit, thanks to the teaching of the artists Filippo Agricola, Tomaso Minardi, Vincenzo Camuccini and Cesare Mariani. The triumphal arch, also known as the Arch of Galla Placidia, suffered severe damage in the fire, but cannot be considered a mere 19th-century replica of the original, since something of its authenticity

The canopy by Arnolfo di Cambio, placed over the altar of St. Paul's tomb, is supported by four columns of red porphyry.

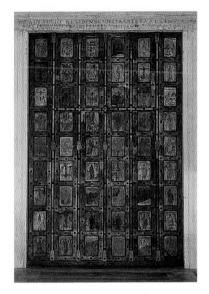

and beauty were preserved. The style of its mosaic decoration can be compared with that of San Marco in Venice; it shows Christ in the center with his hand raised in blessing in the Greek manner (thumb and third finger joined together, the others extended) between two angels and the 24 elders of the Apocalypse. The Apostles Peter and Paul are shown below, the latter apparently pointing down towards his tomb.

The canopy of 1282, the earliest work by Arnolfo di Cambio in Rome, placed over the papal altar and the *Confessio* (the holiest of places, being the spot where the saint was buried), suffered minimal damage in the fire. While it was being dismantled, restored and replaced in its original position, it was discovered that the artist had used pieces of marble with early Christian carvings. The four porphyry columns support four small trefoil arches surmounted by pediments and pinnacles. In the middle, with its graceful decorations, stands a kind of miniature bell-tower, and niches in the corners contain small statues of Sts. Peter, Paul, Luke and Benedict. Located on the outside spandrels are small statues of St. Timothy, Paul's favourite disciple, and of Abbot Bartholomew, the head of the monastery between 1282 and 1297, who commissioned the work. He is shown offering the canopy to St. Paul. Visible at the side of the ogees are some small bas-reliefs, and pairs of angels support the elegant tracery rose-windows. The relief motifs of the canopy are inspired by ancient art, while the vertical thrust of the pinnacles and of the four small lateral arches is typically Gothic. In the right-hand transept, not far from the canopy, is the famous candlestick, standing more than five meters high, the tallest of all the marble columns used in the Middle Ages to hold the Paschal Candle on Holy Saturday.

The candlestick is important not only for its liturgical and public functions, but also as a symbol of Christ "tree of life and light of the world," as he appears in

The Byzantine door situated so that it closes off the Holy Door.

Madonna and Child: on August 22, 1541, St. Ignatius Loyola took his vows before this image, thus laying the foundations for the Society of Jesus.

iconography, inscriptions and the liturgical context for which the candlestick was created. Here sculpture, which, according to the conventions of Romanesque art, must decorate but not alter the functional form, is subordinate to architecture. Its imposing size gives it a monumental unity, even though it mixes classical and vernacular stylistic devices.

The candlestick is divided into eight segments: a base with fantastic creatures, one segment containing carved plant and animal motifs, the next three depicting scenes from the Easter liturgy, followed by one characterized by intertwined vegetation, then by eight monstruous figures, and lastly by the cup that holds the candle. Six themes are represented: Christ before Caiaphas, Christ being mocked by soldiers, Pilate washing his hands, the Crucifixion, the Resurrection and the Ascension. Of these the most interesting is the Crucifixion, in which Christ appears wearing a *colobium* (tunic) and in the Byzantine posture of *patiens* (suffering), with the two thieves shown much smaller, and behind, the two large figures of the Virgin and St. John supporting the arms of the Cross. They symbolize the way all humanity shares in the Divine Sacrifice, according to an iconographic theme which established itself towards the end of the Middle Ages. The various segments were produced by several artists, Pietro Vassalletto and Nicola d'Angelo among them.

At the far end, to the left of the transept, the altar of the Conversion of St. Paul, by Camuccini, is a permanent reminder of one of the Apostle's most fundamental experiences: his *metanoia*, or inner transformation. At its sides are the statues of St. Gregory the Great and St. Bernard.

Further ahead is the Chapel of Santo Stefano, also connected with St. Paul's conversion, as a reminder that, before his conversion, Paul had taken part in the stoning of the young saint.

The marble wall decoration used in part materials from the early basilica; above the altar stands the statue of the first martyr.

The Chapel of the Blessed Sacrament, built in the original Baroque style to celebrate the 1625 Jubilee, contains the 14th-century wooden crucifix that survived the fire. On the right stands

Chapel of the Blessed Sacrament, executed by Carlo Maderno, burial place of the painter Cavallini. Above the altar is the miraculous wooden crucifix of St. Bridget.

The ancient candlestick whose purpose is to hold the Paschal Candle is the work of Nicola d'Angelo and Pietro Vassalletto (20th century).

the wooden statue of St. Paul, scratched by the pilgrims who wanted to take splinters away with them as relics. There is also a mosaic of the Virgin and Child dating from the 12th or 13th century, like the mosaic in the apse.

The mosaic in the apse (circa 1220) altered the appearance of the basilica. The restoration of 1836 faithfully followed the original iconography: the enthroned Christ holds a book in his hand; on his left are St. Peter and the Apostle St. Andrew, and on his right are St. Paul and St. Luke the Evangelist. The other Apostles appear in the lower level.

The prostrate figure at Christ's feet is that of Pope Honorius III. His portrayal in that posture changes the Roman tradition, in which the Pope was placed symbolically on the same level as the Apostles and the saints. This difference confirms that those responsible for the mosaic were Venetian artists of the beginning of the 13th century, inspired by Byzantine models.

On the occasion of the 1625 Jubilee, Carlo Maderno (1556–1629) left his mark on the rectangular Chapel of San Lorenzo, placed on the end wall of the basilica, restructuring nd emphasizing the space around the altar.

Following the fire, the precious marble pavement was laid in 1852. It is in this chapel, also known as the Chapel of the Choir, that the Benedictine monks celebrate the Lauds, Vespers and Mass that form the core of the Benedictine liturgy. On the altar of Our Lady of the Assumption, placed against the

THE CLOISTERS

The cloisters were started in 1205 and completed between 1235 and 1240, almost certainly by the Vassalletto family, the Roman marble workers who built the cloisters at San Giovanni in Laterano. A double series of small columns, straight, octagonal or twisted, some with mosaic inlay, support rounded arches above which runs an entablature decorated with polychrome marble and mosaic. Many fragments of the ancient basilica have been collected there, including a Roman sarcophagus with bas-reliefs. On the upper level of the monastery, four elegant rooms house a museum with an important collection of Christian inscriptions and tombstones.

right-hand transept, is preserved a mosaic copy of the *Coronation of the Virgin* by Giulio Romano (1492), and a precious altar top, covered in malachite and lapis lazuli, a gift from Tsar Nicholas I.

View of the cloisters with twisting columns in the foreground.

SAN GIOVANNI IN LATERANO

Some scholars say that in the 4th century there was a *domus ecclesiae* on the site of the present basilica. This *domus ecclesiae* had been constructed out of the house of Fausta, wife of Constantine, and turned into a Christian basilica with adjoining buildings by Pope Melchiades (311–314) in 313. The Emperor had given him the building, and the Pope immediately had the hall, in what had been the adjacent house owned by the Laterani (a Roman family who had lived on the southern side of the Coelian hill during the Empire), turned into a church. The font, the second oldest after the one in the catacombs of Pontianus, was constructed from a monumental fountain in the ancient palace. Constantine thus chose to build the first church of the new religion on the outskirts of the city, near the Aurelian Walls and the Asinaria Gate, so as not to antagonize Rome's still large pagan population. However, another suggestion is that the *domus ecclesia* was built directly on top of the ruins of the house of the Laterani; discovered beneath it are what are believed to have been the remains of a building dating from the Severan period (192–235), later used as barracks for the Emperor's personal guard, i.e. the *equites singulares*. Constantine had the barracks demolished after dissolving the guard, which was loyal to Maxentius, whom he had defeated at the battle of the Milvian Bridge in 312, and built the early Christian basilica.

At first it was dedicated to the Saviour; later, during the papacy of Gregory I (590–604), it was also dedicated to Sts. John the Baptist and John the Evangelist. Pope Lucius II gave it its present name in 1144.

The colossal marble head of Constantine (Emperor 306–337), from the basilica of Massenzio, is now in the Palazzo dei Conservatori in Rome.

The Church of San Giovanni in Laterano, in an engraving by Giuseppe Vasi (1752).

The early building was very similar in plan to the present one, with five naves, separated by splendid marble columns. The transept was limited to the three central naves; the two shorter ones on either side ended in two square chambers that extended beyond the side walls.

The basilica was richly embellished with gold and marble, and was thus called "golden"; papal archives record Constantine's generous donations of these materials. Legend also has it that in it were preserved the Ark of the Covenant, the Tablets of the Law, the Golden Candelabrum, the Tabernacle and Aaron's priestly robes. The high altar was situated in the crossing, with the papal throne directly in line with it. The widest and highest of the central naves rested on 30 columns of yellow Numidian marble, probably of the

SACROSANCTA LATERANENSIS ECCLESIA OMNIUM URBIUM ET ORBIS ECCLESIARUM MATER ET CAPUT
(Most holy church of the Lateran, mother and foundation of the churches of all cities and of the world). This church alone has this title. It was the first Christian basilica in Rome and in the world, thirteen years older than the Vatican basilica, both the seat of the papacy until the 14th century and the seat of the Bishop of Rome.

same length as those underneath the 18th-century organ.

The arches were decorated with panels of the same marble, and there were mosaics with a gold background. The dominant color was yellow, and this may be why it was called "golden." The side naves were supported inside the perimeter wall on 40 columns in green Peloponnesian marble; these were shorter and needed large plinths to

bring them up to the slope of the ceiling, with an arch supporting a wall that was pierced to let light through. The basilica suffered many disasters over the course of the centuries, and just as many operations to repair and alter it. In 455, Vandals under Genseric ransacked the church and stole all the priceless treasures it contained. It was restored by Pope Leo the Great (440–461). A few centuries later, in 896, it suffered considerable damage in an earthquake, and Pope Sergius III (904–911) commissioned extensive works to reinforce it, and also had the gallery decorated with mosaics.

Further restoration and decoration was carried out in the 12th century under Alexander III (1159–1181), who had the east façade built (now lost), and Clement III (1187–1191), who decorated it with mosaics (also

---

HISTORICAL EVENTS

The most important events include the five Ecumenical Councils of 1123, 1139, 1179, 1215 and 1512. It was in this very basilica that in 1133 Pope Innocent II crowned King Lothair III of Germany as Emperor Lothair II. In 1223, Charles of Anjou was crowned King of Sicily, and in 1312 Henry VII of Luxemburg was made Emperor. In 1347 the newly knighted tribune and reformer Cola di Rienzo proclaimed the *lex regia*. Pope Eugenius IV entrusted the basilica to the care of the secular clergy, who ran it from 1450. The Chapter, which takes precedence over that of St. Peter's in all the great church ceremonies, includes a Cardinal archpriest and 22 canons.

---

lost). Nicholas IV (1288–1292) added further sumptuous decorations, including the large mosaic in the apse, the work of Jacopo Torriti and Jacopo da Camerino.

The apse of San Giovanni had a choir ambulatory, that is, a semicircular processional path in the style of the early Christian cemetery basilicas, the only example of this rare feature in early medieval Rome. The existing 12th-century throne, by Nicola d'Angelo, a Roman worker in marble, was placed in the primitive apse.

In 1308 the basilica was partially destroyed in a fire and immediately rebuilt by Clement V (1305–1314).

CHRONOLOGY			
313 Constantine gives the land belonging to the Laterani to Pope Melchiades		**455** The church ransacked by Vandals under Genseric	**896** The chu damage an eart
314-18 The church of five naves built			
300	400		800
	324 The basilica consecrated by Pope Sylvester I and dedicated to the Saviour	**c. 457** The church restored by Pope Leo the Great	**904** The rebu unde Serg

One of the fifteen statues on the façade of San Giovanni in Laterano.

THE PRIMITIVE BASILICA

The primitive basilica, in severe style, was dedicated to Christ the Saviour, because an image, described in Greek as "*acheiropoieta*," or "not made by human hand," is traditionally said to have miraculously appeared during the consecration of the church built by order of Pope Sylvester I in 324. The image was then reproduced in mosaic on the façade, and was considered miraculous throughout the Middle Ages.

After another fire in 1361, restoration work was carried out under Popes Urban V (1362–1370), who was responsible for the canopy over the papal altar, and Gregory XI (1370–1378). Pope Martin V (1417–1431) had the celebrated marble masons of the Cosmati school make the polychromatic pavement, and Pope Eugenius IV (1431–1447) commissioned the architect Filarete to deal with a series of restorations. Under Innocent VIII (1484–1492) the arch in front of the papal altar was built, and under Pius IV (1559–1565), the east façade and the ceiling; the ceiling was later gilded by order of Pius V (1566–1572).

The front of the basilica had three windows with pointed arches and showing an image of the Redeemer, and was preceded by a portico with six columns. The Patriarchate adjoined the basilica; the Pope's seat was, in fact, the Lateran basilica, and under the influence of Constantinople it was changed from an *episcopium* into a *patriarchium*. The Pope was attended by seminarians chosen from among the pupils of the *orphanotrophium* or *schola cantorum*, the former at San Paolo fuori le Mura and the latter at St. Peter's, or by lay people from the city's noble families who took seats in the raised pews (*cubiculari*). For about a thousand years, from its foundation until the beginning of the 14th century, the basilica of San Giovanni in Laterano and the

1000	1300	1500	1600	1700	1800

1144 The church dedicated to St. John

1300 The first Holy Year declared

1308 The church destroyed in a fire

1377 The Popes return from Avignon

1586 Domenico Fontana executes the north façade

1732 A competition to build the main façade is announced

c. 1878 Pope Leo XIII has the apse rebuilt

1361 The church burned down for the second time

1562–1567 Pirro Ligorio plans the wooden ceiling

1309 The papacy transferred to Avignon

1646 Borromini rebuilds the interior

1732–1740 Alessandro Galilei executes the façade

Reconstruction of the ancient façade of San Giovanni in Laterano.

THE LEGEND OF THE BASILICA'S FOUNDATION

The founding of the basilica is associated with the legend of Constantine's leprosy. Sts. Peter and Paul appeared to him in a dream, telling him he would be cured if he was baptized. So Constantine sent for Pope Sylvester I (314–335), who baptized him and his leprosy was cured. He then had the church built as a sign of his gratitude.

buildings that sprang up around it were the seat of the papacy. In addition, when it became the cathedral of Rome, it took precedence over the basilicas of St. Peter and San Paolo, made sacred by their apostolic relics. However, when it was decided to move the papal residence to Avignon, in France, from 1304 to 1377, San Giovanni in Laterano was abandoned, and on their return to Rome, the Popes chose to settle first in Santa Maria in Trastevere and then ultimately in the Vatican.

Sixtus V (1585-1590), seeing the dreadful state the church was in, decided to have some major restoration work done. He commissioned his trusted architect, Domenico Fontana, to build the Lateran Palace as a papal summer residence, in what was then open country.

Later, however, the Quirinal hill seemed a more suitable location, perhaps because of its strategic position. This meant that the Lateran Palace lost all its magnificence, and was left abandoned until the middle of the 17th century.

BORROMINI'S RESTORATION

Innocent X placed Francesco Borromini in charge of restoring the basilica four years before the Jubilee of 1650, and the work was completed in 1649. The most beautiful of the three designs was selected and five large arches were opened, separated by pairs of huge pilasters, between which 12 niches were located, later filled by statues of the apostles. On the sides of the upper part of the nave, rectangular windows above the arcades alternate with paintings set inside oval frames. The wooden ceiling was kept, although the architect had intended to build a barrel vault.

St. Leo the Great restored the basilica after its sacking by the Vandals in 455. The pope is portrayed by Raphael in one of the frescoes in the Room of Heliodorus in the Vatican.

Interior of San Giovanni in Laterano, with its
sumptuously decorated floor and ceiling.

Visit

In 1732 Pope Clement XII Corsini (1730– 1740) announced a competition to build a new façade for the basilica. The contest led to heated controversy, but it was important because it demonstrated the different styles of 18th-century church architects. The winner was Alessandro Galilei, from Florence, who started work that same year. Instead of following Baroque conventions, he went back to the monumental style of the late Renaissance. His stunning façade, preceded by a short flight of stairs, has a single order of pilaster strips and engaged columns, divided laterally into three sections, the one in the center standing proud of the rest, and five bays.

The tall pilaster strips and the two pairs of columns supporting the triangular pediment rest on a tall stylobate, or base, and have Corinthian capitals. Above the portico, with its architrave and five openings, is a loggia, also consisting of five arches, of which the central one is a large Palladian window. The entablature, with a balustrade running the entire length of the façade, is

PRACTICAL INFORMATION

Piazza San Giovanni in Laterano, 4.

☎ 06 69 88 64 33.

🚌 3, 16, 81, 85, 87, 186, 650, 850 and other routes serving Piazza San Giovanni.

🚊 3.

Ⓜ A San Giovanni.

Opening hours: church: 7 a.m.–6:30 p.m.; cloisters 9 a.m.–6 p.m.

Museum 9 a.m.–1 p.m., Mon–Sat.

Admission fee for cloisters and museum.

✝ 📷 🔊

The Corsini Chapel, built in 1734 by A. Galilei above an ancient cemetery.

The baptistery, often restored, is from the era of Constantine. Its present octagonal form, from the 5th century, was a model for baptisteries throughout the Christian world.

THE LENGHT OF THE BASILICA

The length of the basilica is 130 meters, 1.5 m longer than Constantine's original basilica of St. Peter's. The central nave is 16 meters wide and 87 long.

THE EGYPTIAN OBELISK

The Egyptian obelisk at the center of the square is the tallest (47 meters including the base), and the most ancient in Rome, which has 13 obelisks, more than any other city in the world.

The Pope alone may celebrate Mass at the papal altar. Its Gothic canopy, with frescoes, dates from the 14th century.

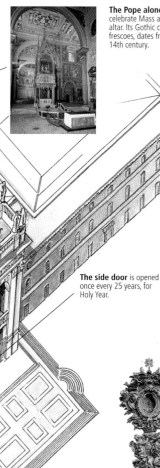

The side door is opened once every 25 years, for Holy Year.

Statues of Christ, the two St. Johns and the Doctors of the Church

Reliquary of Clement XII (1730–1740), preserved in the museum of San Giovanni in Laterano.

THE FAÇADE

The competition held in 1732 to build the present façade was won by Alessandro Galilei. A total of 23 architects, who submitted 27 original wooden models of their finished design, took part.

adorned with fifteen colossal statues: in the center stands the Redeemer, between St. John the Baptist and St. John the Evangelist; they are flanked by the twelve Doctors of the Greek and Latin Churches, representing the doctrinal unity of the Church of Christ. Galilei no longer accepted the pictorial or chiaroscuro values of the various elements offered, but instead set himself the problem of perspective as a measure of elegance and taste. In fact, the proportional relationship between the first and second levels is entirely new, since the lower part is extended lengthwise while the upper has the usual dimensions.

This very original solution was necessary because the new façade looked down a long, straight street, the Strada Giulia, making it difficult to view it from the front. The architect therefore extended his design sideways, greatly enlarging the lower part and using the steps up to the entrance to increase the effect.

The bottom level of the portico, reached by one of the great wrought iron gates, has a low barrel vault with stucco coffers, and in the center the arms of Clement XII. The five doors correspond to the five naves, and the central door has priceless authentic bronze panels, taken from the ancient Curia in the Roman Forum. It is believed that if an expectant mother touches them, she can hope to give birth to a boy.

The last door on the right, defined as the Holy Door, is opened only once every 25 years, for the Jubilee, by removing the wall behind it. The ritual was performed for the first time in this basilica by Martin V in 1423 and later extended

CLEMENT XII'S RELIQUARY

The precious reliquary above the altar of the Sacrament contains a fragment of the table at which Jesus and the Apostles are said to have eaten the Last Supper. The relic is shown on Easter Sunday.

to the other Roman basilicas. The basilica is 130 metres long and has five naves, with a wide transept and a huge apse, completely rebuilt during the pontificate of Leo XIII (1878–1903). Its architecture and decoration go back to the work done by Borromini and its many statues and paintings clearly express his key idea: the Church, whose cornerstone

The great bronze doors at the basilica's main entrance.

is Christ, is built on the foundation of the Apostles and the prophets. The wooden ceiling is the original one from the 16th century; it was probably designed by Pirro Ligorio between 1562 and 1567 and is decorated with the coat of arms of Pius IV dei Medici, during whose papacy the work was carried out. Nearer the front wall are the coat of arms of Pius VI Braschi (1775–1799), who had the ceiling repaired.

In the central nave, in niches set in the pilasters, are statues of the Apostles, made in the early 1700s. Located above the niches are the high-reliefs in stucco of Scenes from the Old and New Testaments, executed in the 16th century by Alessandro Algardi and his collaborators, who created a "biblical concordance," that is to say, the life of Jesus the Messiah, as prefigured in the Old Testament.

Higher up, in oval stucco frames, are portraits of the prophets, painted in the late 1600s or early 1700s.

A number of chapels open off the outermost side aisles. The second on the right is the 19th-century Torlonia Chapel, in the form of a Greek cross with a dome, one of the latest chapels of the Roman aristocracy. The third on the right, the Massimo Chapel, was built by Giacomo Della Porta in 1590; it has a crucifix by Sermoneta (1575) on the altar. The first on the left, the Corsini Chapel, was built by Alessandro Galilei between 1732 and 1735. The tomb of Clement XII, however, is the work of Giovan Battista Maini. The third chapel on the left, from the early 1600s, is by Onorio Longhi, and the fourth was built by Giovanni Antonio De Rossi in 1675.

The transept was completely rebuilt

The façade of the Lateran basilica with the statues of Christ the Redeemer, St. John the Baptist, St. John the Evangelist and the eight Doctors of the Latin and Greek Church.

provided by Charles V of France. It is the work of Giovanni di Stefano; the twelve panels, painted by Barna da Siena in 1367–1368, were restored and retouched about a century later by Antoniazzo Romano and Fiorenzo di Lorenzo.

Up above, behind a metal grille, are a set of 19th-century reliquaries (replacing the 14th-century originals), which contain relics of the heads of St. Peter and St. Paul. Under the canopy is the papal altar. Only the Pope is allowed to celebrate Mass here. It is modern, but it encloses the ancient wooden altar used until the 4th century by the first thirteen Popes, from St. Peter to St. Sylvester. In the *Confessio* under the altar, the tomb of Martin V Colonna by Simone Ghini (1443) is worth noting.

Borromini's most extraordinary achievement was his refurbishment of the tombs of the Popes and Cardinals which were in the old basilica.

to a design by Giacomo Della Porta during the papacy of Clement VIII (1592–1605). Its important frescoes were painted by well-known late 16th-century Mannerist artists under the direction of the Cavalier d'Arpino. High up at the far end of the right arm of the transept is the organ, dating from 1598. Opposite, in the left arm, is the richly decorated altar of the Sacrament, made to the design of Pier Paolo Olivieri in 1600. The Colonna Chapel, built by Girolamo Rainaldi in 1625, also opens off the transept and has beautiful wooden stalls adorned with statues of saints. To the right of the chapel, under the 20th-century monument to Leo XIII, is the entrance to the sacristy. In it is an *Annunciation,* painted by Marcello Venusti in 1555 after a design by Michelangelo, and on the altar a late 16th-century *Magdalene,* attributed to Scipione Pulzone. In the center of the transept is the Gothic canopy, made during the papacy of Urban V (the Frenchman Guillaume de Grimoard), using funds

The Torlonia Chapel, designed in the late Neoclassical style by A. Raimondi (1830–1850), is dedicated to St. John Nepomucene.

Papal throne from the 5th century preserved in the cloisters. It has a seat dating from classical antiquity, and spiral columns, and is the oldest papal throne in existence.

Innocent X had ordered that once the work of reconstruction was completed, the tombs, or parts of them, were to be rebuilt inside the restored church; the tombs were therefore dismantled and moved to the cloisters when reconstruction began.

When Cardinal Fabio Chigi was elected Pope in 1655, as Alexander VII, Borromini was able to act more freely. He kept a fragment of each tomb and inserted it into the new monument he had designed, using the medieval fragments like relics to be preserved in their new setting, in perfect harmony with the style he was imposing on the renovated church. And since there were oval windows in the outside walls of the side naves, and the funerary monuments could not be placed against them, Borromini incorporated them into the new tombs, so that they appeared to be elements of the design itself. He personally worked to vary motifs and aesthetic solutions, in order to give the faithful real evidence of the centuries-old religious life of the Lateran basilica, as if presenting an ideal collection of mementos from the past.

A fragment of a fresco by Giotto has been incorporated into the monument of Boniface VIII; it shows the Pope proclaiming the first Holy Year (1300). It can be dated to the period immediately before the Assisi frescoes, which, as we recall, include the *Dream of Innocent III,* showing the

ancient basilica with a typical Romanesque bell-tower. In the center of the tomb of Sergius IV, who died in 1012, is a bas-relief of the Pope giving a blessing, inserted into a frame by Borromini formed of the stars that appear on the coat of arms of Alexander VII Chigi.

Leaving the basilica by the door at the far end of the right arm of the transept, we note the external façade of 1589, by Domenico Fontana, superimposed on the old façade, of which the surviving entablature and the two side bell-towers can be seen. The upper of its two orders of five

The statue of St. Andrew, with those of Sts. Peter, John, James, Bartholomew and Simon, is located in the left aisle.

façade, with the identical motif of blind arches aligned with the architectural order of the ground level, is connected to the rest of the Palatine chapel of the Patriarchate (the Scala Santa). Passing along the left wall of a 19th-century construction built by Leo XIII, the visitor reaches the 4th-century baptistery, the earliest of its kind and the only known example in Rome. Sixtus III (432–440) had it completely rebuilt on an octagonal plan, using eight porphyry columns that had been cut but not used, and adding an atrium. Pope Hilarius (461–468) instead had three chapels built, two of which survive, though with radical alterations. The one farthest to the left, with the original bronze doors made by Umberto da Piacenza in 1196, is dedicated to St. John the Evangelist. Its original mosaic of birds and flowers still adorns the vault. The second chapel, on the opposite side, retains its door panels, taken from the Baths of Caracalla; silver was used to cast them, and they "sing" when opened. The chapel is dedicated to St. John the Baptist and was built by Pope Hilarius in the 5th century to be used by "the people of God," as the inscription tells us. The third chapel, originally dedicated to the Holy Cross, but now to Sts. Rufina and Secunda and Sts. Cyprian and Justina, is architecturally the most important. It contains a 5th-century mosaic and, above the door, a *Crucifixion* in high relief of the school of Bregno (1492). A fourth chapel, now dedicated to St. Venantius, was added by John IV (640–642) in the 7th century, and

arches, called the "Loggia of Benedictions," was frescoed by a group of Mannerist painters working under the direction of Cesare Nebbia and Giovanni Guerra. The loggia is joined to the Lateran Palace, just as the Pulpit of Boniface was to the Patriarchate. In the same way, the

THE CLOISTERS

The cloisters, reached through a door at the far end of the left aisle, are a masterpiece of Cosmatesque art. Small arches rest on pairs of small columns, of different forms and with different capitals. The cloisters, on a square plan, were built between 1225 and 1236 by members of the Vassalletto family. In the center of the cloister is a 9th-century well-head. The vaults of the ambulatories rest on columns with Ionic capitals, of a later date. The four porticos contain many fragments of the ancient basilica. The most beautiful of these are the remains of the episcopal throne of Nicholas IV (1288–1292), once in the apse, a 5th-century stone head of a woman, believed by some to be a portrait of St. Helena, and the 13th-century tomb of Cardinal Annibaldi della Molara, attributed to Arnolfo di Cambio, other parts of which are now in the church itself.

View of the cloisters of San Giovanni with the twisting columns in the foreground.

PLAN OF THE BAPTISTERY

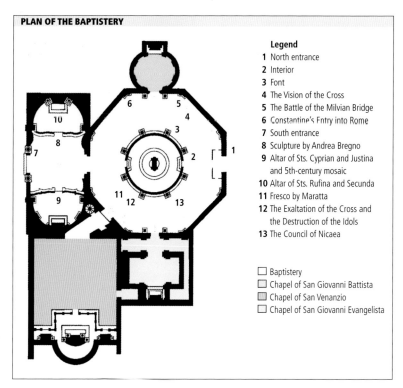

Legend

1 North entrance
2 Interior
3 Font
4 The Vision of the Cross
5 The Battle of the Milvian Bridge
6 Constantine's Entry into Rome
7 South entrance
8 Sculpture by Andrea Bregno
9 Altar of Sts. Cyprian and Justina
   and 5th-century mosaic
10 Altar of Sts. Rufina and Secunda
11 Fresco by Maratta
12 The Exaltation of the Cross and
   the Destruction of the Idols
13 The Council of Nicaea

☐ Baptistery
☐ Chapel of San Giovanni Battista
▨ Chapel of San Venanzio
☐ Chapel of San Giovanni Evangelista

still has its magnificent 16th-century wooden ceiling.

It was perhaps these two chapels, built in honour of St. John the Baptist and St. John the Evangelist, that later gave the adjoining basilica, originally dedicated to the Saviour, its present name. The Baptistery was called "St. John *ad vestes et ad fontem*," words that refer to the baptismal ritual: *vestes* to the neophytes' white robes, *fontem* to the water in which the catechumens were immersed.

Paul III (1534–1549) had the dome,

which was dilapidated, demolished, and the present lantern, with its sloping roof, built.

The Lateran Palace, built on the site of the ancient Patriarchate, was the papal residence from the time of Constantine until the flight to Avignon (1305) and was destroyed,

View of the exterior of the baptistery.

THE BAPTISTERY

The Lateran baptistery is in the form of an octagonal structure, with brick walls. Its glazed windows bear the arms of Pius XI, who was responsible for the excavations of 1925. The outlines of windows blocked up when various restoration works were carried out can be seen in the walls. The dome has eight oval windows.

with the basilica, in the fire of 1308. When the Popes returned from Avignon in 1377 they were forced to transfer the Holy See to the Vatican. Then in 1586, Sixtus V Peretti had Domenico Fontana destroy almost all that remained of the old fabric, comprising the Loggia of Benedictions and a number of venerable medieval chapels attached to the basilica, in order to build a summer palace for the papal court. Only Constantine's basilica, the early Christian baptistery and the most significant medieval chapel, the Sancta Sanctorum ("Holy of Holies"), were preserved.

The Patriarchate had consisted of a group of buildings that extended as far as Pope Leo's *triclinium*, or dining room, and were joined to the oratory of St. Lawrence, called the Sancta Sanctorum. Facing the palace stood the equestrian statue of Marcus Aurelius, which Sixtus IV had returned to that spot. In the portico was an oratory dedicated by Pope John XXII to St. Thomas for use as a papal sacristy, in which numerous relics were housed. From the right-hand nave of the church a grand staircase led to the council chamber, which was the same length as the

THE BAPTISMAL FONT
The font was arranged so that water entered through the figures of seven silver stags, later carried away by barbarians. In the early Christian era, it contained only a few centimeters of water, since immersion was, and is, symbolic.

modern front of the palace of Sixtus V, with ten apses, and a dais at the back. On the side facing the piazza to the north, the chamber ended in a covered loggia, built by Boniface VIII for the great Jubilee of 1300. On the wall of this loggia Giotto painted the imposing fresco of which a fragment was placed inside the church and currently forms part of Pope Boniface's monument.

The principal entrance to the great palace faced the Chapel of the Sancta Sanctorum, where a great number of relics were housed, and from where a

The lost loggia of Boniface VIII, or *Pulpitum Bonifacii*, shown here in a drawing by Martin van Heemskerck, was connected to the Patriarchate by a series of blind arches.

magnificent stair, covered by an imposing vault, led to the central part of the palace. There, on the right, stood the tower of Zacharias, near which was another entrance to the palace, in the form of three staircases (the middle one being the Scala Santa), leading to the oratory of St. Sylvester and then to that of St. Lawrence.

In a lunette in the Vatican Library Cesare Nebbia (1585–1590) painted the scene at the ceremony of the Jubilee promulgated by Sixtus V in the same place as that of Boniface VIII. As the old Patriarchate disappeared shortly afterwards, this picture is the only precious evidence we have of it. In it can be seen the side façade of the basilica, without the porticos that later covered it. On the left is the palace with the council chamber built by Leo III (its side apses can be seen), and outside one can pick out the *Pulpitum* or Loggia of Boniface VIII, with the front of the Patriarchate

behind it. To the left is the oratory of St. Sylvester, and that of the Scala Santa with its little portico.

Sixtus V himself never hid the fact that he thought of the Lateran basilica as the most important church in Rome, nor that its papal palace should be refurbished to make it a comfortable and dignified setting for the Curia, suitable to house not only the Consistory but also, for extended periods, the papal administration and the Cardinals. Therefore, in designing the great building of the Lateran Palace, on a square plan and placed against the side of the basilica, Fontana was inspired by the Palazzo Farnese, completed by Michelangelo. From an aesthetic standpoint, it is interesting to note the contrast between the solid wall, with its powerful angular rustication, barely joined to a slender molded string course, and the open loggia-cum-belvedere, which can be seen rising above the roof with columns in the open and receptive to the varying

The ancient baptismal font, located in the center of the baptistery.

Pope Sixtus V had the Loggia of Benedictions demolished.

at the base of the obelisk of Theodosius).

The Loggia of Boniface, from which was read the bull heralding the first Christian Jubilee, was altered under Pius IV, and demolished by Domenico Fontana in 1586, by order of Sixtus V, and replaced by the present north portico.

Sixtus V transferred the most solemn event of the ecclesiastical year from the Vatican to the Lateran: this even was the Easter blessing *urbi et orbi*. The rebuilding of the Lateran was completed at the start of the summer of 1590, shortly before the Pope died, and it is hard to determine what he intended to do. We do know, however, that the Lateran was then designated the main ecclesiastical complex in Rome.

The Scala Santa and the Sancta Sanctorum are located close to the basilica of San Giovanni. In 1586, when Sixtus V decided to build the present Lateran Palace, he assigned the architect Fontana the task of

effects of light and shade. The balustrade, formed of pierced Cosmatesque parapets with a spread-eagle as for a lectern, is enriched by the color of the different marbles. The functional solution of the centrally aligned column emphasizes the architect's freedom of invention, which is consistent with his overall purpose. From the symbolic point of view, one can see how the ancient Imperial heritage has survived. In fact, the meaning of the glorifying arch of the tabernacle that covers the altar, of the canopy, the loggia and the vault of the gallery under which, in late antiquity and the Byzantine period, the Emperor would be seated with inflexible ceremony, is well known. It is interesting to compare the concept of the *Pulpitum Bonifacii* with the Imperial Palace of Constantinople, which overlooked the hippodrome (depicted in a relief

The ceiling of the Hall of the Seasons, which was probably the throne room.

Loggia of the piano nobile, which extends on three sides and was the area set aside for the Pope's private apartments.

separating the chapel from the Patriarchate and making it more monumental. He also ordered that access to the Sancta Sanctorum should be created by using the grand staircase of the old palace, which consisted of 28 marble steps. From the middle of the 15th century it was identified with the stair of the *Praetorium* of Pontius Pilate, the stair climbed by Jesus during his trial; hence its name Scala Santa ("Holy Stairs").

The architect completed the operation of moving the Scala Santa to the Sancta Sanctorum in a single night. Ever since then, the Scala Santa and the Sancta Sanctorum, the Christian shrine of shrines, facing the Lateran Palace, have formed a single whole. At the top of the stair, through a small window with a grating, the faithful can just see the old papal chapel which houses the *acheiropoieta* image ("not made by human hand") of the Saviour, and the most important collection

of relics of the Roman martyrs (now in the Vatican Museums). That is what gives the place, the Popes' ancient private chapel, its sacredness. Entry is via the atrium of the papal chapel, decorated with groups of marble statues, including the Ignazio Jacometti's *Kiss of Judas* and *Ecce Homo* (1854). In the center, flanked by four other stairs, is the Scala Santa. Those not performing the minor pilgrimage, climbing the stair on their knees, to commemorate Jesus' ascent to be tried before Pontius Pilate, can reach the Sancta Sanctorum via the stair on the right, and go through a bronze door with ancient locks. The

In the Sistine Hall of the Vatican Library is a fresco by Cesare Nebbia, circa 1588, showing the new Lateran Palace of Sixtus V. The palace was completed a little before the Pope's death. Only the Constantinian baptistery and the basilica were left out of the reconstruction.

chapel was an innovative building in terms of its architecture and decoration. The walls of its single bay, with a small rectangular apse and a Gothic vault, divided into four by ribs, are partly covered in pieces of ancient marble. The mosaic ceiling (1278) is a veritable gem of Cosmatesque art. The symbols of the four Evangelists appear in the four sections. On the wall above the altar, the kneeling Nicholas III, flanked by Sts. Peter and St. Paul, offers a model of the chapel to Christ enthroned, with two angels.

At the entrance are two scenes representing the martyrdoms of Sts. Peter and Paul. In the crucifixion of St. Peter, the cross becomes a symbol of contradiction: on the left are the soldiers, on the right the grieving women, and in the background a selection of Roman monuments. The background to the beheading of St. Paul is the desolate area of Tre Fontane, with the Church of San Paolo on the right. The blood of Christ thus flows symbolically in the martyrdom of the first of the Apostles, and Rome becomes the New Jerusalem, an image of the divine city. Facing the altar we see the stoning of St. Stephen and the martyrdom of St. Lawrence. At the side is the beheading of St. Agnes and St. Nicholas providing dowries for three poor girls. On each wall, the triangles with lunettes, between the rectangle of the scene and the curve of the figure, contain figures of angels, eight altogether. The rest of the space, at the sides of the windows, is occupied by large vases, from which emerge the stems of

View of the exterior of San Giovanni in Laterano.

Salus populi Romani. Four silver lamps burned constantly beside it. Sts. Peter and Paul stand on either side and in the next lunettes, Sts. Agnes and Lawrence; Sts. Nicholas and Stephen. Three lighted lamps are depicted on the west wall. A shield bearing a bust of Christ appears in the mosaic of the little vault, gloriously supported by four flying angels. Under the canopy is an altar still preserving precious relics which, with the *acheiropoeita,* make this papal chapel the holiest sanctuary of any in the Western world.

plants, curled into three spirals. On the lower level, around the walls, are 28 niches containing standing figures from the time of Sixtus. They represent the Virgin, the Apostles and saints. On the wall of the altar, two niches, protected by a grating, give the effect of a reliquary.

Two porphyry columns support the architrave of the choir, which bears the inscription *Non est in toto sanctior orbe locus* ("There is no holier place in the whole world"), marking the sanctity of the spot, and framing the miraculous (*acheiropoeita*) image of the Saviour, placed behind the altar inside a silver reliquary with relief figures, made in the time of Innocent III. This icon, said to be a true image of the Saviour, traditionally started by St. Luke and completed by the hand of an angel, was the holiest of those in Rome. Every year, on 15 August, and also at times of great calamity, the Popes would carry it in procession to Santa Maria Maggiore, to "visit" the image of the Virgin, the

THE CANOPY OF SAN GIOVANNI IN LATERANO

The canopy of San Giovanni in Laterano. Only the celebrant was able to get a complete view of the canopy above the altar, where precious relics are still kept and which refers back to the Ark of the Covenant (Exodus 25:22). Similarly, the porphyry columns and the architrave have the effect almost of a pergola. It is a symbolic visual language that runs all the way through the monument, resplendent with Cosmatesque marble and described as "the holiest place in the entire world" (*Non est in toto sanctior orbe locus*).

THE PAPAL CHAPEL

The Papal Chapel was built in the time of Constantine and later rebuilt by Nicholas III (1277–1281). It was given the name of the Roman martyr St. Lawrence, but became known as the Sancta Sanctorum, a pious conflation of the innermost part of the Temple of Jerusalem with the chapel of the Popes. Just as the Holy of Holies of the Old Testament contained the Ark of the Covenant, and was visited once a year by the high priest, the Palatine Chapel contained the icon of the Saviour in Majesty, the miraculous *acheiropoieta*, protected by silver doors, and a precious collection of relics of Christ, the Virgin, Sts. Peter and Paul, and St. Agnes. In Rome, as in Jerusalem, no one but the Pope was allowed to officiate in the Sancta Sanctorum, where he performed the evocative Good Friday service.

The Scala Santa, situated on the east side of Piazza San Giovanni in Laterano, is one of the remnants of the old Lateran Palace.

The interior has 28 steps, believed to be those climbed by Christ when he appeared before Pontius Pilate.

SANTA MARIA MAGGIORE

This patriarchal basilica, built on the Esquiline hill, stands at the end of Via Merulana, formerly Gregoriana, widened and straightened by Pope Gregory XIII (1572–1585) to link it directly with the Lateran. The church harmoniously combines work from different periods, from Christian antiquity to the Baroque.

Consequently, the structure of three naves with columns bearing architraves, and part of the mosaic decoration, are basically the 5th-century originals. The Cosmatesque marble pavement and the Romanesque bell-tower are medieval, the coffered ceiling dates from the Renaissance and the two domes and the external elevations from the Baroque period. Research carried out from 1966 to 1972 shows that the earliest part of the church goes back to the time of Sixtus III (432–440). The mosaic dedication at the top of the arch reads *Xystus episcopus plebi Dei*, "Pope Sixtus to the people of God," and building is

The basilica of Santa Maria Maggiore,
in an 18th-century print.

believed to have been started not earlier than about 420, perhaps by demolishing the church of Pope Liberius (if it ever existed). However, discovered six meters below the level of the present church were the remains of a sewer and part of a street, dating from the middle of the 1st century AD, set inside a courtyard with a portico, on whose walls, corresponding to the apse of the church, a mural calendar was painted in the 3rd or 4th century. A few fragments survive, showing work done on the farm in each month of the year. In

front of the basilica of Sixtus was a four-sided portico (for some it was merely a narthex) reduced to a single portico under Eugenius III (1145–1153), as recorded in an inscription still visible in the right-hand courtyard of the church. The portico was redesigned under Gregory XIII (1572–1585).

Following the building phase under Sixtus, in the 7th century a crypt was added to the church, in which the relics of the Grotto of the Nativity, from Bethlehem, and a fragment of what was traditionally held to be Jesus' cradle are said to have been

THE LEGEND OF THE SNOW

According to a legend of which there is no written record until the first half of the 13th century, Mary is said to have appeared in 352 to Pope Liberius and to the patrician John, a high-ranking figure. She invited them to build a church on a spot where snow had fallen, even though it was midsummer. The incident happened on the night of August 5, on the Cispian summit of the Esquiline hill itself. This defined the area where the church was to be built, and it was said to have been paid for by John and his wife.

To commemorate the event, every year on that date a shower of white petals falls from a hole made for the purpose in the ceiling of the church, during a solemn service.

It is also referred to in documents as the "Liberian" church, or "St. Mary of the Snow," although, since no trace of the structure remains, the precise spot on which Liberius may have built his church is still a matter of dispute. Sources suggest that it was situated "next to the market of Livia," which can actually be located, outside the Esquiline Gate, near the Arch of Gallienus, still preserved today.

The statue of the Virgin and Child, at the highest point of the façade of Santa Maria Maggiore, the most important of the churches dedicated to the Virgin.

preserved. For these reasons, until the Carolingian era the basilica was also known as St. Mary of the Crib. Pope Paschal I (817–824) had the sanctuary raised. It was previously the same height as the naves, from which it was divided only by screens. Nicholas IV had a polygonal apse built between 1288 and 1292, further back than the existing one, and a transept; so what was previously the arch of the apse became a triumphal arch.

In 1673, under Pope Clement X (1670–1676), Carlo Rainaldi refurbished the exterior of the apse, and between 1740 and 1750, on the order of Benedict XIV (1740–1758), Ferdinando Fuga added a new façade, connecting it to the medieval mosaic façade.

"The mosaics of Santa Maria Maggiore, i.e. the arch, the nave and the frieze on the entablature, form one of the supreme examples of 5th-century art" (L. Barroero). They are the oldest surviving iconographic cycle from an early Christian place of worship.

The dominant theme of the mosaics in the triumphal arch is the mystery of the Incarnation of Christ, showing episodes relating to the birth and childhood of the Saviour, taken from the canonical Gospels and also from apocryphal texts. Episodes from the Old Testament, portrayed in the central nave, also present events from the lives of the great patriarchs and precursors of Christ, and are thus linked to the main theme of the Incarnation. The theme of devotion to the crib was repeated in the oratory next to it (now lost), intended to reproduce the setting of Christ's birth, and in a wonderful *Nativity* by the sculptor Arnolfo di Cambio. Another dominant idea, especially in the original decoration of the apse, of which the arch survives, is the Divine Motherhood of Mary, proclaimed at

CHRONOLOGY

300–500 AD		600–700	800–1100	
420 Work probably started	**432-440** Sixtus III completes the church		**1075** Pope Gregory VII abducted by his opponents while celebrating Christmas Mass in the basilica	
352 The Virgin appears to Pope Liberius and invites him to build the church		**600** The chapel containing the relics of the Bethlehem Grotto added	**817-24** Paschal I has the sanctuary raised	**1288-92** Nicholas IV adds the apse and the transept

The *Confessio* was rebuilt in 1864 by V. Vespignani, with a silver urn by L. Valadier to contain the relics held to be those of the crib of Bethlehem (in the photograph).

the Council of Ephesus in 431. Santa Maria Maggiore was one of the first churches to be dedicated to the Virgin after that date. The intention was to reveal Mary as the preordained instrument of the Incarnation of the Saviour. Hence, this idea recurs, and idea that was particularly relevant in an age tormented by doctrinal controversy.

1347	1590	1673
Cola di Rienzo crowned tribune in Rome	The Sistine Chapel of Domenico Fontana completed	Carlo Rainaldi rebuilds the apse

1400–1500	1600–1700

1378	1743
Rebuilding of the bell-tower completed in the papacy of Gregory XI	Ferdinando Fuga adds the façade, on the orders of Benedict XIV

THREE POPES FOR A RESTORATION

Three Popes contributed to the rebuilding and restoration of the basilica. Gregory XIII (1572–1585) made alterations to the 12th-century portico; Clement X (1670–1676) had Carlo Rainaldi redesign the outside of the apse; Benedict XIV (1740–1758) commissioned Ferdinando Fuga to design the façade we see today.

Gregory XIII in a portrait by Lavinia Fontana.

Visit

Ferdinando Fuga's stunningly dramatic façade, with five openings in the portico and three in the loggia, includes both the medieval elevation and the central part of the mosaics of Filippo Rusuti, executed at the end of the 13th century and depicting Christ enthroned blessing, in a shield supported by angels, the Virgin and saints on the left, and other saints on the right. In the lower tier, various incidents from the Miracle of the Snow, with Pope Liberius and John the patrician, are depicted on panels with captions. Of the three entrances in the façade, the one on the left is the Holy Door, opened only, like those in the three other principal basilicas, on the occasion of a Jubilee. Four large angels, in marble and gilded bronze, made by Pietro Bracci in 1749, and originally placed on top of the canopy above the altar, are now situated on top of the loggia. Outside the façade are various 18th-century statues of saints and Popes, in addition to the Madonna and Child. The reliefs decorating the portico, inspired by events connected with the basilica, are also from the first half of the 18th century.

The interior measures approximately 70 by 35 metres and is harmonious. Its three naves are divided by 40 Ionic columns with capitals standardized by Fuga; however, previously they were different one from another, like their bases. It was originally lit by many windows, some of them closed up in the 16th century. In the spaces created between them, late Mannerist frescoes were painted, showing stories of the Virgin and Christ.

Above the architrave, decorated with a stucco frieze and mosaics from the era of Sixtus III, are 36 5th-century mosaic panels along both walls, showing scenes from the Old Testament, which were framed by small stucco shrines with a tympanum above them. Some of the panels were heavily restored by painting, while others were reconstructed in 1593 and later. Six were lost at the end of the 16th century, to make the large entrance arches to the Pauline and Sistine chapels. Without following a precise logical order, scenes drawn from the stories of Abraham, Isaac and Jacob, in a style that still shows classical influences, are depicted on the left,

PRACTICAL INFORMATION

Piazza di Santa Maria Maggiore.
☎ 06 69 88 68 00.
🚌 16, 70, 71, 714.
🚋 14.
Ⓜ A and B Termini, B Cavour.
Opening hours: 7 a.m.–6:45 p.m. every day. 🚻📷

The Coronation of the Virgin, Jacopo Torriti (1295), is the central image of a series of mosaics in the apse.

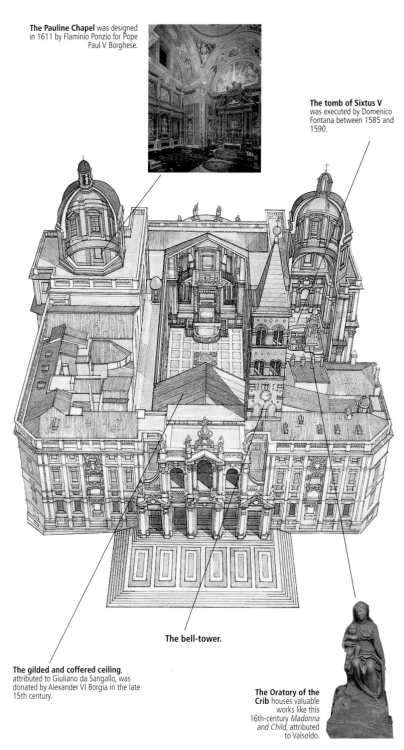

The Pauline Chapel was designed in 1611 by Flaminio Ponzio for Pope Paul V Borghese.

The tomb of Sixtus V was executed by Domenico Fontana between 1585 and 1590.

The bell-tower.

The gilded and coffered ceiling, attributed to Giuliano da Sangallo, was donated by Alexander VI Borgia in the late 15th century.

The Oratory of the Crib houses valuable works like this 16th-century *Madonna and Child*, attributed to Valsoldo.

on the altar is the venerated image of the Madonna "Salvation of the Roman People" (*Salus populi Romani*), painted by a Byzantine artist of much-debated chronology and traditionally attributed to St. Luke. Pope Clement VIII and Pope Paul V are buried here, and members of the Borghese family in the crypt below. Two smaller chapels are dedicated to St. Charles and St. Frances of Rome. Next to it is the oval Sforza Chapel, completed by Giacomo Della Porta in 1573 to a design by Michelangelo. Of almost the same date is the Cesi Chapel, possibly by Guidetto Guidetti, which can be dated to 1550, containing funerary monuments by Guglielmo Della Porta. Benedict XV had the monument to the Queen of Peace erected in the same nave.

In the semicircle of the apse, lit by four flared windows, is a mosaic made by Jacopo Torriti between 1288 and 1292, showing the coronation of the Virgin by Christ, on a blue tondo with stars, in front of a row of angels. The donors include Pope Nicholas IV, on the left, and Jacopo Colonna, on the right, with saints. Among them, we can observe St. Francis, intended to be associated with Nicholas, who was the first Franciscan Pope.

In the spaces between the windows are scenes from the life of Mary, dated to the end of the 16th century. The mosaic on the arch of the apse was restored in the 20th century. It shows the 24 elders of the Apocalypse adoring the Lamb of God, and the symbolic cities of Jerusalem and Bethlehem. The transept houses

and from those of Moses and Joshua on the right. The gilded and coffered ceiling, which Vasari considered the work of Giuliano da Sangallo, was donated by Alexander VI Borgia at the turn of the 15th century. Tradition has it that it used the first gold brought from America by Columbus and given to the King and Queen of Spain. It replaces the original trussed roof, and its decoration was sensitively reworked in the 18th century.

A portion of the pavement is the Cosmatesque original, a gift of the Roman aristocrats Giovanni and Scoto Paparoni during the papacy of Eugenius III (1145–1153). The Pauline, or Borghese, Chapel was designed by Flaminio Ponzio between 1605 and 1615 for Pope Paul V. It was built in the area occupied by the old sacristy, with its entrance from the left-hand nave. It is a Greek cross, and the pictorial decoration was executed between 1610 and 1612 by various artists, including the Cavalier d'Arpino and Guido Reni. Located

The dome of the Pauline Chapel was realized by Domenico Fontana in 1586 for Pope Sixtus V.

frescoes, partially revealed in 1931, with images of the prophets in medallions, attributed to Pietro Cavallini, Cimabue, Filippo Rusuti and the young Giotto.

On the current triumphal arch the mosaic showing scenes from the childhood of Jesus is instead composed very freely with sumptuous colors: the tesserae are of 190 different shades. While the Nativity as such is not shown, one can see the Annunciation, with Mary enthroned, spinning purple wool according to an apocryphal tradition, the Presentation in the Temple, the Gifts of the Magi, the angel appearing to St. Joseph in a dream, a representation of the Governor Afrodisius receiving the Holy Family on the Flight into Egypt, in the city of Sotine, taken from Pseudo-Matthew, the Massacre of the Innocents and the Magi before Herod. At the top of the arch, the empty throne of Christ

The interior of the basilica, divided into three naves by 40 Ionic columns, boasts a precious marble Cosmatesque pavement and a Renaissance coffered ceiling.

Christ Enthroned among Angels forms part of the mosaics on the façade, created by Filippo Rusuti at the end of the 13th century, and frequently restored since.

(*hetoimasia* in Greek) refers to the Second Coming of the Redeemer, on Judgement Day.

In the sanctuary, the canopy by Ferdinando Fuga (circa 1740) features columns of porphyry and bronze. A stairway leads to the *Confessio*, made in the second half of the 19th century by Virginio Vespignani. The silver and crystal urn containing the supposed relics of the cradle from Bethlehem is kept on the altar. In front of it is a statue of Pius IX praying, which dates from 1883. Among the funerary monuments, that of Clement IX, in the right nave, from 1671, and that of Nicholas IV, designed by Domenico Fontana in the mid-16th century, are especially of interest.

From the right nave, facing the Pauline Chapel, the Sistine Chapel, or Chapel of the Blessed Sacrament, can be reached; this was executed by Domenico Fontana between 1584 and 1590, for Sixtus V, on the plan of a Greek cross, with a large central dome, two small side chapels and the Pope's tomb. The marble decoration on the walls comes from a classical monument from the time of Severus, the Septizodium, a monumental façade situated at the foot of the Palatine hill.

On the side walls are the funerary monuments of Sixtus V and Pius V (the "victor" at the Battle of Lepanto, which he marked by promulgating the short prayer Maria, *Auxilium Christianorum*), to the right and left

respectively, also by Fontana. The pictorial decoration is for the most part Late Mannerist.

In the center, a small staircase leads to the oratory of the Crib, restored by Arnolfo di Cambio (1289) and brought here in 1590 from the first crypt, which was probably behind the apse or near the sanctuary, by Domenico Fontana. Nonetheless, he wished to preserve the original setting, which was meant to evoke the Grotto in Bethlehem. Inside, the figures of the prophets David and Isaiah, on the pinnacles of the arch at the entrance, are attributed to Arnolfo, as are the figures of the Nativity, i.e. the three Magi, St. Joseph, the ox and the ass, except for the Madonna and Child, who are in a niche.

Arnolfo's work forms part of the projects initiated by Nicholas IV and Cardinal Jacopo Colonna. Visible on the pavement, next to the columns of the central nave, is the simple tombstone of the Bernini family, under which also lies the famous Neapolitan architect, sculptor and painter, Gian Lorenzo Bernini.

Visible on the right wall, near the right-hand entrance to the transept, is the Gothic tomb of Cardinal Consalvo Rodríguez (1299),

The **bell-tower** is the highest in Rome, at 75 meters. Romanesque in style, with polychromatic decoration, it was rebuilt in 1370–1378, during the papacy of Gregory XI, on existing foundations. It has been considerably altered over the centuries, and in the 16th century a pyramidal spire was added.

Sacristy of the Canons, with frescoes by Passignano, from 1608. From here one enters the Chapter House, previously the "Hall of the Washbasin," with 15th-century reliefs, brought here from the demolished papal altar by Mino del Reame.

From the baptistery one can also enter the 15th-century Chapel of San Michele and San Pietro in Vincoli, with the arms of Cardinal Guillaume d'Estouteville, and a pavement in Cosmatesque style. The surviving fragmentary frescoes have been attributed to Piero della Francesca. On either side of the basilica are two palaces: the one on the right was built in 1605 by Flaminio Ponzio, under Paul V. The one on the left, which imitates it in style, is dated later, and was completed by Fuga in 1735.

with its excellent Cosmatesque decoration by Giovanni di Cosma, and, in a trilobate arch is a mosaic of the Madonna with saints. From the right-hand nave again, one reaches the baptistery, formerly the Chapel of the Winter Choir, built in 1605 to a design by Flaminio Ponzio, but redesigned in 1825 by Giuseppe Valadier.

Noteworthy among the funerary monuments in this area is that of Odoardo Santarelli, by Alessandro Algardi, which can be dated circa 1640. From the right-hand side one enters the

View of the baptismal font.

The statues of the three Magi form part of the *Nativity* of 1289, executed by the sculptor Arnolfo di Cambio.

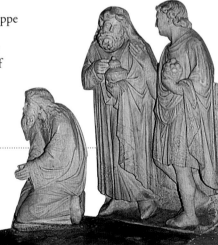

SANTA CROCE IN GERUSALEMME

The basilica rises up on the slopes of the Esquiline hill, a place associated with memory and the meditation on Christ's Passion. It was founded by Constantine the Great and his mother, St. Helena, on a site occupied by a Palatium, property of the Empire, referred to as "Sessorianum," perhaps signifying *auditorium*, during the papacy of St. Sylvester I (314–337). Although it was called Basilica *Heleniana* or *Sessoriana*, its official name was *Hierusalem*. The name referred specifically to the Relic of the Cross and the other Relics of the Passion of Our Lord, miraculously discovered on Calvary and brought to Rome by the Emperor's elderly mother. But it also links Rome with Jerusalem, an association reinforced by the crucifixion of St. Peter. The name Santa Croce in Gerusalemme was adopted at the start of the early Middle Ages.

According to tradition, Pope Gregory the Great appointed a Cardinal priest incumbent of the basilica, and over the centuries it was renovated several times under Popes Gregory II (715–731) and Adrian I (771–795). The funerary inscription of Pope Benedict VII (975–984), next to the main entrance, says that because the church was so rich in relics in the tenth century a set of buildings designed to house canons was constructed alongside it. No canons were appointed, however, and in 1049 Pope Leo IX placed it in the hands of the Benedictines of Monte Cassino. When they moved to San

STUDY THE CROWN OF THORNS

"If something good loses its savour, then turn at once to the Crucifixion (...) and study the crown of thorns, the nails, the spear between his ribs. Gaze upon the wounds in his feet and his hands, on his head, in his side, his whole body. Remember how much he loved you who so suffered for you, who endured so much for you, who bore so much for you. Believe me, who seeing such a thing, found all things joyful (...) by virtue of the passion of Christ" (St. Bonaventure, "On the Perfect Religious Life," in *Five Mystical Works*).

Statue of St. Helena in Santa Croce. Two inscriptions in her honour, dated to the beginning of the 4th century and found near the church, confirm that the Holy Empress had a residence here.

Santa Croce in Gerusalemme, façade commissioned by Pope Benedict XIV (1743).

Sebastiano in 1062, Pope Alexander II installed the canons regular of San Frediano of Lucca, and during the reign of Pope Lucius II (1144–1145), they rebuilt the basilica in Romanesque style. They created three naves, added a bell-tower with double- and triple-arched openings, and built a portico in front of the fourth-century façade. The complex remained deserted throughout the Avignon papacy, until Pope Urban V handed it over to the Carthusians around 1370.

They in turn carried out important restoration work, especially while the Spanish Cardinal priests Pedro Gonzales de Mendoza (1484–1493) and López de Carvajal (1495–1523) were incumbents of the basilica.

In 1561, after the Carthusians were transferred to Santa Maria degli Angeli, in the Baths of Diocletian, Lombard Cistercians from the congregation of San Bernardo took over. They still preside over the basilica. One of their first projects, under Cardinal Francisco Pacheco, was the building in 1570 of the Chapel of the Relics, while Pomarancio was commissioned to paint a series of frescoes depicting the story of the *Finding of the Cross*,

in the Chapel of Sant'Elena.

Santa Croce's appearance today is the result of its reconstruction as a Baroque church between 1741 and 1744 as ordered by Pope Benedict XIV Lambertini. The work was commissioned to two architects,

Rome-born Domenico Gregorini and the Sicilian Pietro Passalacqua. Town planning works were also carried out at the same time. Monte Cipollaro was levelled, and roads linking Santa Maria Maggiore, San Giovanni in Laterano and Santa Croce, which stands at the end of the axis of Via Felice, built by order of Pope Sixtus V at the end of the 16th century, were completed.

The prestigious Sessorian Library, housed in a stunning gallery built between 1724 and 1727 by the architect Sebastiano Cipriani, with frescoes by the painter Gian Paolo Pannini, of Piacenza, belongs to the monastery.

Until 1871, when it was taken over by the Italian State, the library held the famous Fondo Sessoriano, a collection now in the Biblioteca Nazionale Centrale in Rome. It consisted of over 450 valuable manuscripts and printed books, and was founded by Abbot Ilarione Rancati in the mid-17th century. The present scenographic and lively façade replaces the old medieval one.

CHRONOLOGY

						1740-58 The basilica is remodelled in Baroque style under Pope Benedict XI
	715-795 Restoration work carried out during the papacies of Gregory II and Adrian I		**1049** Pope Leo IX hands the monastery over to Benedictines from Monte Cassino		**1561** The Lombard Cistercians take over	
300	**700**	**1000**	**1300**	**1500**		**1700**
320 d.C. Constantine and his mother, Helena, found the Hierusalem basilica		**1144-45** The church is remodelled in the Romanesque style	**1370** Pope Urban V assigns the church complex to the Carthusians	**1570** The Chapel of the Relics built		

Hemisphere of the apse, detail of the cycle showing the *Finding of the Cross: The Cross of Christ captured by Chosroes.*

Sets of pilaster strips divide it into three concave and convex bays, under a curved pediment topped by a decorative tympanum, and by balusters and statues. Below, three doors open into an oval atrium with a domed vault, its surrounding ambulatory decorated with groups of pilaster strips and columns. Eight ancient granite columns, four on each side, alternate with six pilasters dating from the eighteenth-centur renovation, dividing the interior into three naves. On the wooden false vault that carries the arms of Pope Benedict XIV is the painting *St. Helena Ascending into Heaven* by Corrado Giaquinto, dated to 1744. Located in the sanctuary is an eighteenth-century canopy, and below the high altar a wonderful basalt urn containing the remains of Sts. Caesarius and Anastasius. Another painting by Giaquinto, *Apparition of the Cross on the Day of Judgement*, is in the vault. The semicircular apse has a cycle of frescoes of the *Holy Cross Found by St. Helena and Recovered by Heraclius*, and above them, within a mandorla formed of cherubim, one of *Christ Blessing*, attributed to Antoniazzo Romano and dated to 1492. Also worth noting are the Romanesque

The Titulus, one of the relics preserved in Santa Croce, bears a part of the inscription "Jesus of Nazareth King of the Jews."

The Chapel of the Relics. In 1570, on the authority of Pius V, the relics were moved from the underground Chapel of Sant'Elena to a location above so as to protect them from dampness. Because of the increasing numbers of pilgrims, it was decided to build the present Chapel out of the former sacristy, to a design by Florestano Di Fausto, inaugurated in 1930 and finished in 1952.

87

frescoes in the gable, a twelfth-century Cosmatesque pavement, and seventeenth- and eighteenth-century paintings in the side aisles by Raffaele Vanni, Luigi Garzi, Carlo Maratta and Giuseppe Passeri. The funerary monuments include that of Cardinal Quiñones, erected in the 16th century to a design by Jacopo Sansovino.

Very important to pilgrims are the two semi-subterranean chapels linked with the basilica by two flights of steps on either side of the sanctuary, one at the entrance, the other at the exit. On the right is the Chapel of Sant'Elena, on the left the much later Chapel of the Pietà.

The holy Empress Helena sprinkled earth from Calvary on the floor of the first chapel, which bears her name and is also called the *cubiculum Sanctae Helenae*, after which she placed the precious Relic of the Cross there. It is known that the Emperor Valentinian III (425–455), with his mother Galla Placidia and his sister Honoria, had the vault decorated with sumptuous mosaics, of which no trace remains. The mosaic was completely renewed at the turn of the 6th century by Baldassare Peruzzi, based on a design by Melozzo da Forlì, and since being restored in 1995 it can be admired in all its glory.

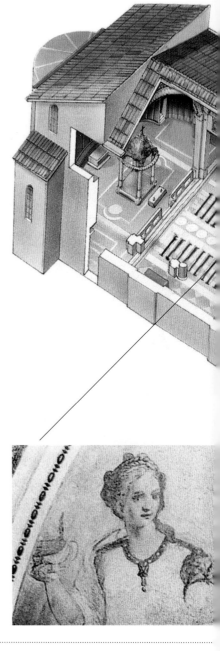

PRACTICAL INFORMATION

Piazza di Santa Croce in Gerusalemme, 12.

06 706 130 53.

16, 81, 649, 810.

3.

Opening hours: 7 a.m.–7 p.m.

The Chapel of Sant'Elena is decorated with frescoes depicting the Virtues.

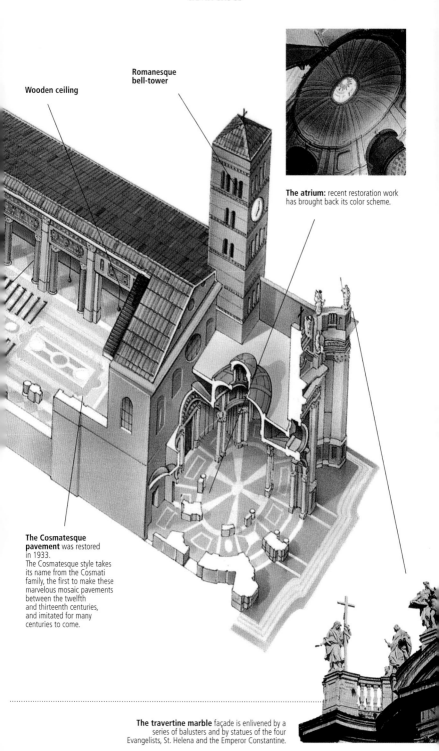

Romanesque bell-tower

Wooden ceiling

The atrium: recent restoration work has brought back its color scheme.

The Cosmatesque pavement was restored in 1933.
The Cosmatesque style takes its name from the Cosmati family, the first to make these marvelous mosaic pavements between the twelfth and thirteenth centuries, and imitated for many centuries to come.

The travertine marble façade is enlivened by a series of balusters and by statues of the four Evangelists, St. Helena and the Emperor Constantine.

damaged by the humidity in the chapel, they were removed in 1724 and then sold. They are currently in Grasse, France.

The Chapel of the Pietà, or Gregorian Chapel, was built between 1495 and 1520 according to the wishes of Cardinal Bernardino López de Carvajal, as a mirror image of the Chapel of Sant'Elena, and connected to it. The name evokes the love of God, and may refer to the pity of God the Father who sacrifices his Son,

In the center is the figure of Christ blessing, surrounded by the Evangelists and four events from the Crucifixion. Frescoes showing the *Finding of the Cross* were painted on the area below the mosaic by Nicolò Circignani, called Pomarancio, in 1590. The statue of St. Helena above the altar is a copy of the Vatican Juno, conveniently adapted by the addition of the symbols of the Passion. In 1602 Rubens painted three canvases for this chapel: *St. Helena with the Holy Cross*, the *Crucifixion* and *Christ Crowned with Thorns*. As the paintings were

WE SHOULD LOVE ALMIGHTY GOD

"The Son of God came down into the world and became flesh, he suffered on the cross, he has redeemed us from our imprisonment, he has made glorious our humanity. For God has loved not only the just but also the sinners, and he has sent his Son to die for us that we might burn with ardent love for him. We should love Almighty God because he created us, but even more so because he has redeemed us. We should love him because he has given us being, but even more so because he has saved us through the death of his Son, so that we may enjoy for all eternity the life of the blessed. Let us love God because he loves us" (St. Bernard, *The Word and the Soul: Daily Meditations*).

THE RELICS

Besides the relics recorded to have existed in ancient times (three fragments of the Cross, a nail from the Crucifixion, the Titulus and two Thorns from the Crown), other relics, all believed to support the teachings about the Passion, are preserved in the basilica. These include the horizontal limb of the cross of the Good Thief (St. Dismas), a digital bone of St. Thomas, and fragments of the Pillar of the Scourging, the grotto of the Crib and the Holy Sepulchre. In the early days, the list of relics such as these also included a coin belonging to Judas, the sponge soaked in vinegar and the rock on which Christ sat when he pardoned Mary Magdalene.

and of the Son of God who sacrifices himself, or to the pity of humanity, for whom the sacrifice is made, for him who makes it. Divine pity, as an act of grace, is different from human pity, which is a feeling of love or compassion.

The Chapel of the Pietà, on whose altar a marble bas-relief of the *Dead Christ Lying in Mary's Lap* (1628–1629) was placed, is connected to the altar of St. Gregory. This is a precious reliquary in the form of a triptych, with a silver frame, doors that open, and some 200 cases. A late thirteenth- or early fourteenth-century mosaic of

The high altar of Santa Croce expresses the link between the celebration of the Eucharist and the sacrifice of Good Friday.

the *Imago pietatis*, portraying the Suffering Christ, occupies the center. In the silver frame seven of the ten enamels that were planned have survived. They depict the Scourging, Christ Carrying the Cross, the Crucifixion, and the coat of arms of Anjou, the Holy Sepulchre, del Balzo and Orsini Montfort. The work was probably commissioned by Raimondo del Balzo, who went on a pilgrimage to the Holy Land in 1380, while the donation to the basilica is dated to 1386. A few years later, word spread that the image of Christ was the same one seen by Pope Gregory the Great. The inscription *Fuit Sancti Gregorii Magni Papae* can be read on the tympanum of the reliquary. Tradition has it that as St. Gregory was celebrating Mass in the Basilica Sessoriana, the Christ in Pietà appeared, in the attitude of the *vir dolorum* (man of sorrows). No life of the saint mentions this vision, and the legend is thought to have originated in the basilica itself. An inscription below the *Imago pietatis*, engraved in 1495 by Israel Van Meckenem, supports this suggestion. It reads: "Copy of the holy image of the Pietà which Pope Gregory the Great had it painted in the church of Santa Croce, following his vision." St. Bernard of Clairvaux (1090–1153) was also blessed with the same vision

The **Cosmatesque pavement** inside the church.

The **reliquary** preserved in the Chapel of San Gregorio.

while he was celebrating Mass in the oratory near the monastery of Tre Fontane, in Rome. The vision of St. Gregory was depicted in 1630 on the vault of the Chapel of the Pietà by two artists, Girolamo Nanni, of Milan, a native of Milan who came to Rome in 1620, and the Roman painter Francesco Nappi (circa 1565–1630). The painting expresses the teaching about Purgatory and how souls may be liberated through the prayers of the faithful who appeal to the saints for intercession. St. Gregory and St. Bernard, whose spiritual descendants were responsible for managing the chapel in 1561, are both included. At the center of the vault, starting from the bottom, the scene is that of penitent souls enveloped in the flames of Purgatory. On either side, angels choose two of these souls; their penance now at an end, they set out to follow the tiny soul (*animula*) rising towards the Holy Trinity. St. Gregory the Great, in his papal robes, his tiara next to him, and St. Bernard, with his white cowl and his Abbot's mitre, are shown kneeling in the middle section.

Standing behind St. Gregory we can see St. Benedict of Nursia, and behind St. Bernard, St. Robert of Molesme. Their role is to intercede for souls in Purgatory. Above them are other, more powerful mediators: St. Paul and St. John the Baptist on the left, St. Peter, with the keys of Paradise, and another Apostle, on the right. Between the two pairs of figures is the

The representation of Christ Pantocrator dominates the center of the vault.

Discovery and Triumph of the Cross (detail), attributed to Antoniazzo Romano.

Virgin, in an attitude of supplication before the Trinity, which crowns the composition, her gaze directed towards Christ. The four sections of the vault contain four symmetrical scenes, two facing St. Gregory, two St. Bernard.

In keeping with the Catholic doctrine solemnly reaffirmed by the Council of Trent (*Decree on Purgatory*, 1563), the freeing of souls from Purgatory is associated with the sacrifice of the Eucharist. If this is celebrated at the altar of San Gregorio al Celio the soul enjoys a plenary indulgence and the personal intercession of St. Gregory the Great. A few other altars have the same privilege, including the Gregorian altar *ad instar* in Santa Croce, which dates from 1574. The church was included in the pilgrims' itinerary of Roman churches, and later became a Jubilee basilica. In the mid-16th century it was also included in St. Philip Neri's route of the Seven Churches and it remains today an important religious site for both Rome and the Universal Church.

PILGRIMAGES TO SANTA CROCE
The basilica was, and it is still, often visited by pilgrims, especially during particular times of the liturgical year: September 14 – Exaltation of the Cross; May 3 – Discovery of the Cross; fourth Sunday in Lent – exposition of the relics; Good Friday – papal processions from the Lateran to Santa Croce (since the 8th century).

The Triumph of the Cross, painted by Corrado Giaquinto between 1742 and 1743, measures 6 meters by 4.

The Pietà, bas-relief above the altar, by an unknown early-seventeenth-century sculptor.

SAN LORENZO FUORI LE MURA

Lawrence the deacon, a victim of persecution under Valerian and buried in the catacomb of Cyriaca at Verano, on the Via Tiburtina, was among the martyrs most venerated in Rome. Around 330, Constantine may have erected a small oratory above his tomb, with a double stair so that pilgrims could get there more easily. It is certain that he also built,

at the foot of the hill near the venerated memorial, a large circular cemetery basilica, with curved naves. This structure was called "the Great" and remains of it now lie partly under the modern Verano cemetery. It was not until the second half of the 6th century that Pope Pelagius II (579–590) cut away part of the hill and built a basilica

Funerary monument of Alcide De Gasperi

Ambo or pulpit

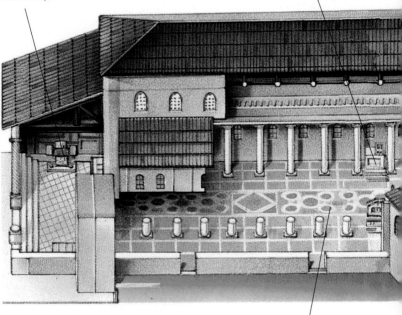

The Cosmatesque pavement is divided into three naves, with a double row of eleven columns.

PRACTICAL INFORMATION

Piazzale del Verano, 3.
 06 49 15 11.
 71, 492.
 3, 19.
Opening hours: 7:30 a.m.–12:30 p.m., 3 p.m.–6 p.m. every day.

The massive bell-tower, featuring eight stories, the upper five of which have pairs of windows, was built in the 12th century.

The canopy, a shrine with four small columns enclosing the high altar, was built in 1148.

The presbytery with the thirteenth-century episcopal chair, used by the popes during the Mass.

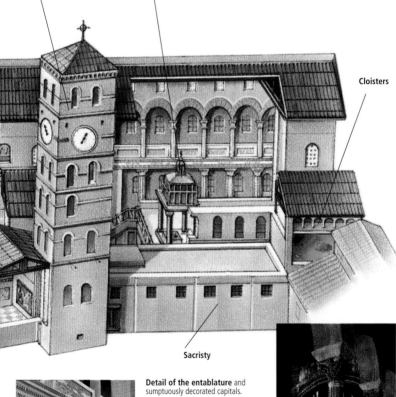

Cloisters

Sacristy

Detail of the entablature and sumptuously decorated capitals.

The interior of the basilica seen from the gallery.

of three naves with internal galleries on the site of the early memorial to the martyr. It was oriented in the opposite direction from the present church, built by Honorius III (1216–1227), to cope with the massive water penetration that was threatening the basilica of Pelagius. Its floor was raised, and it became the sanctuary of the medieval church, which surrounded and enclosed it.

The façade, destroyed by bombing on July 16, 1943, was restored between 1946 and 1949.

The triumphal arch with the sixth-century mosaic representing Jesus with the Saints. To the right, Pope Pelagio with a model of the basilica.

This complex of buildings, in the form of two structures facing each other, is preceded by a narthex by Vassalletto. It has a Cosmatesque pavement, and is divided into three naves with a double row of columns, taken from other sites. Two stairs lead to the raised sanctuary, also in three parts, from which can be seen the mosaic that survives from the apsidal arch of Pelagius church. It shows Christ between Sts. Peter and Paul, with the martyrs Sts. Stephen, Hippolytus and Lawrence, and Pope Pelagius. At the end of the 19th century, the funerary chapel of Pius IX was created in the crypt, decorated with mosaics on a gold background. Also noteworthy is the canopy of 1148, signed by the Roman marble workers Giovanni, Pietro, Angelo and Sasso. The sacristy leads to the late twelfth-century cloisters, the work of Clement III, where there is a collection of sculpture and inscriptions. San Lorenzo, one of the five patriarchal basilicas and one of the Seven Churches on the itinerary of St. Philip Neri, was seriously damaging by bombing in 1943. Many parts of it were restored between 1946 and 1950.

The cloisters, with paired small columns, were probably built by the Cosmati brothers in the 12th century. The monastery to which they belong was expanded in 1190 by the addition of an elegant portico.

CATACOMBS OR SANCTUARIES OF THE MARTYRS

The term "catacombs" refers to the ancient underground Christian cemeteries.

For health reasons, Roman law forbade burials within the city walls, so catacombs are always found outside the city. Contrary to a persistent, but false, belief, they were never used by Christians as places in which to hide from persecution. They served only as underground cemeteries, and any gatherings that took place in them would have had to do with burials, or with the cult of the martyrs buried there. Persecutions were limited to specific periods in the history of the Empire: during the reign of Nero (between 64 and 67 AD), Domitian (in 96 AD),

Decius (249–251), Valerian (253–260) and Diocletian (in the West, mostly between 303 and 305).

The oldest clusters of catacombs date from the late 2nd and early 3rd centuries. Before that, Christians were buried in the same places as pagans, with no segregated burial zones. As Christian communities grew, they needed to create communal cemeteries in order to ensure that all members, however humble, would have a religious burial. Problems of space and the high cost of land were solved by resorting to digging underground, whenever the nature

CHRISTIAN CATACOMBS

❶ San Callisto
❷ San Sebastiano
❸ Domitilla
❹ Priscilla
❺ Sant'Agnese
❻ San Lorenzo
❼ San Pancrazio
❽ Santi Marcellino e Pietro

PRACTICAL INFORMATION

Opening hours: 9 a.m.–12 p.m., 2 p.m.–5 p.m.
Admission fee.

Catacombs of San Sebastiano, cubiculum of the Good Shepherd. It is decorated with paintings from midway through the third century. ❷

Christ the Good Shepherd. The shepherd carrying a lamb is a figure present in pagan art, from archaic Greece onwards.

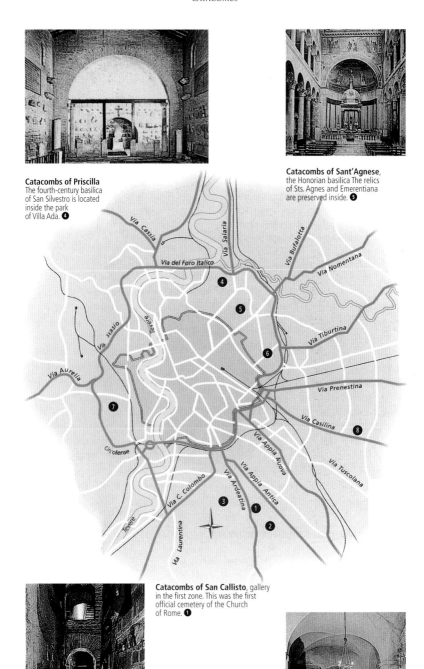

Catacombs of Priscilla
The fourth-century basilica of San Silvestro is located inside the park of Villa Ada. ❹

Catacombs of Sant'Agnese,
the Honorian basilica The relics of Sts. Agnes and Emerentiana are preserved inside. ❺

Catacombs of San Callisto, gallery in the first zone. This was the first official cemetery of the Church of Rome. ❶

Catacombs of San Sebastiano.
The crypt preserves a bust of the saint, attributed to Bernini. ❷

CATACOMBS ABANDONED AND REDISCOVERED

At the start of the 5th century, the custom of burying the dead in the catacombs began to decline, although pilgrims would still visit them as an act of devotion. Between the 8th and the 9th centuries, with the Roman countryside deserted and unsafe because of barbarian incursions, the sanctuaries were gradually abandoned, and the popes decided to move the venerated tombs to the city. The catacombs were rediscovered in more recent times; they were explored by Antonio Bosio (1575–1629) and later studied by the great Roman archaeologist Giovanni Battista de Rossi (1822–1894). Nowadays the Christian catacombs are overseen and cared for by the Pontificia Commissione di Archeologia Sacra (Papal Commission for Sacred Archaeology), which manages and funds, excavations and restoration.

of the rock, which had to be strong yet easy to cut, allowed it. Since Rome was built on a bedrock of soft tufa, this system was widely used, allowing additional burial space to be created by digging several galleries, one on top of another. The catacombs are a system of long corridors galleries, whose walls contain dug-out tombs called *loculi*. Air and light entered through vertical square shafts called *lucernari.* The body would be laid in the cell wrapped in a shroud and the tomb sealed with tiles or marble slabs, on which the deceased's name and date of death would be carved. The latter was called *dies natalis* (birthday), since for Christians, death was the beginning of the afterlife, which is the true life. Opening onto the galleries, besides the cells, were also *arcosolia*, loftier tombs topped by an arch. and family burial chambers, called *cubicula*. A catacomb containing the burial place of a martyr would become particularly famous, and pilgrims would come from all over the Christian world to pay their respects at the venerated tomb.

The tombs of the martyrs have always been well maintained and embellished, in particular by Constantine (306–337) and Pope Damasus (366–384), who wrote his famous inscriptions in verse especially for the martyrs' burials.

ROME AT THE TIME OF THE EARLY CHRISTIANS

Augustus (27 BC–14 AD)	Caligula (37–41)	Claudius (41–54)	Vespasian (69–79)	Trajan (98–117)	
Julio-Claudian Dynasty (27 BC–68 AD)			Flavian Dynasty (69–96)		Antonian Dynasty
	Tiberius (14–37)	Nero (54–68) First persecution of Christians in 65 Sts. Peter and Paul executed in 64 or 67	Titus (79-81) Domitian (81-96) Christian and Jewish philosophers expelled from Rome in 93–94	Nerva (96–98)	Hadrian (117–138)

Giovan Battista de Rossi, the Roman archaeologist who rediscovered the catacombs.

Various special rituals were performed in the catacombs on the anniversaries of the dead. One of them was called the *refrigerium*, or funeral banquet, a pagan custom the Church tolerated within certain limits. The martyrs' anniversaries were also commemorated there, and on those occasions the faithful would gather for the celebration of the Eucharist.

The cemeteries belonged to the Church, which administered them first through the *fossores*, workers who specialized in underground digging, and later through the deacons and presbyters of the city's parishes, called *tituli*.

THE DECORATION

The decoration was simple, mostly made up of frescoes, with subjects derived from pagan art used decoratively or symbolically (for instance, an olive branch, a figure in prayer, or a fisherman). What was really new was the use of subjects from both the Old and the New Testaments: symbols of the catechumen's progress (Jesus in the River Jordan = Baptism), of salvation (Noah in the Ark), of healing (the paralytic and the bleeding woman) and of resurrection (Jonah, Lazarus). These scenes, like pagan paintings from the same period, are framed in narrow red and green lines. In the 4th century, with freedom granted to the Christian religion, the decoration in the catacombs expresses the image of a triumphant Church, with Christ victorious seated among the twelve Apostles.

s Aurelius (161–180) Martyrdom ...stin in 165	Septimius Severus (193–211)	Decius (249–251) Persecution of the Christians	Constantine (306–337) With the Edict of Milan of 313, Christianity is no longer considered unlawful
...5–192)	Severan (193–235)	Diocletian and Constantine (284–337)	
Antoninus Pius (138–161) ...modus(180–192) Victor I Bishop of Rome 189–192	**Caracalla** (211–217) Calixtus Bishop of Rome 217–222	**Diocletian** (284–305) Numerous measures against Christians.	**Constantius Chlorus** (305–306) The year 306 marks the end of the persecutions in the Western world.

The dove and the figure in prayer, two recurring images in the catacombs.

The entrance to the catacombs of Sant'Agnese.

Catacombs of San Callisto

These catacombs are situated two to three miles down the Via Appia Antica, in a location already widely used for pagan burials. They form a very large system, made up of overground as well as underground cemeteries from the end of the second century. Originally separate, they were eventually connected to create a single vast network of communal catacombs. At the beginning of the 3rd century the cemetery was the property of the Christian community, and was regarded as the principal cemetery of the Church of Rome. Pope Zephyrinus (199–217) entrusted its management to his principal deacon, Calixtus, after whom it was named. By the end of the early Middle Ages, the catacombs had been forgotten, and were rediscovered by the archaeologist Giovanni Battista de Rossi, who began his excavations in 1849.

The burial complex consists of an area above the surface, and the actual catacombs underground. There were many buildings at ground level: funerary enclosures, pagan and Christian mausoleums, and a basilica, now lost, dedicated to St. Cornelius by Pope St. Leo the Great.

The Arch of Drusus and the Porta Appia, also called Porta di San Sebastiano, in an old engraving.

The first level, 6–7 meters from the surface.

The second level is the largest; because it contained the venerated tombs, it was here that the faithful wished to be buried.

The third level, 25–26 meters deep.

The "cubicula of the Sacraments," so called because of the paintings that refer to the Eucharist and Baptism.

The crypt of Melchiades, excavated in the 4th century, was dedicated to Pope St. Melchiades, who was Pope Eusebius' successor, and persuaded the Emperor Maxentius to restore to the Church all the property confiscated in 303.

The tomb of Cornelius, where Pope Damasus had one of his beautiful verse inscriptions placed.

Oil lamps were used for lighting.

The crypt of Santa Cecilia, next to the crypt of the Popes, held the body of the martyr St. Cecilia, an object of devotion in the early Middle Ages.

The eastern and western *tricore* (funerary buildings with apses on three sides) have survived. In the floor of the western *tricora* a multiple burial was discovered, later identified as the tomb of Pope Zephyrinus, Calixtus' predecessor, and of St. Tarsicius. The eastern *tricora*, originally the mausoleum of a wealthy Christian, contains a collection of sarcophagi and, as of 1994, the tomb of Giovanni Battista

de Rossi. The first zone is one of the oldest areas, and contains the crypts of the Popes and St. Cecilia. Originally, two parallel galleries were created, each served by a stair. Later excavation created a grid of galleries on a rectangular plan. Opening onto one of the galleries are the "cubicula of the Sacraments," so-called because of painted scenes referring to Baptism and the Eucharist, which date from the early 3rd century, and are among the earliest examples

of Christian painting. The crypt where almost all the Popes of the third century were buried is in this area, and nearby is the crypt of St. Cecilia, an object of devotion in the early Middle Ages.

The crypts of Lucina and the tomb of Pope St. Cornelius (251–253), who died in exile in Civitavecchia

POPES BURIED IN THE CATACOMBS OF SAN CALLISTO

Zephyrinus (199–217)	Anteros (235–236) Cornelius (251–253)	Stephen (254–257)		Caius (283–296)	Melchiades (311–314)
198–228	**229–258**		**259–288**		**289–314**
Pontianus (230–235)	Fabian (236–250)	Sixtus II (257–258) Lucius (253–254)			Eusebius (309–310)

Painting of a banquet in one of the cubicula of the Sacraments.

and was buried in an underground chamber next to the Via Appia Antica, are also very ancient. It was originally separate from the cemetery administered by Calixtus, but the Roman matron Lucina, who owned it, later allowed the Christian community to use it. This is where the tomb of Cornelius, embellished by Pope Damasus, is found, with its Byzantine paintings of Cornelius and his close friend St. Cyprian, Bishop of Carthage. The crypts named after Lucina, decorated with very early paintings, are also located here.

A third, also originally separate zone is that of Pope St. Eusebius (309). Its crypt has the inscription by Pope Damasus mentioning the interesting question of the *lapsi* (those who denied their faith when facing martyrdom). In front of it is the spacious double *cubiculum* of Pope St. Caius (283–296), and, nearby, the *cubiculum* of the martyrs, possibly from the time of Diocletian, Calocerus and Parthenius.

Moses makes water come forth from the rock.

The Via Appia Antica.

Catacombs of San Sebastiano

In time this cemetery, originally called *ad catacumbas* (near the area of subsidence) because of the pozzolana earth extracted there and used for cement in local building, was given the name of St. Sebastian, the martyr who is buried there. The burial ground remained accessible throughout the centuries, and the term "catacombs" has been extended to refer to all underground Christian cemeteries. Another name for the same complex is *memoria apostolorum*, meaning "memory of the Apostles," because for a certain period of time Peter and Paul were venerated there. The area has been intensively used since the 1st century AD, and built upon in various ways throughout different historical periods. The basilica was built in 1608 as ordered by Cardinal Scipione Borghese, by completely rebuilding the existing fourth-century basilica, and making use of its central nave. Flaminio Ponzio was placed in charge of the work and it was completed by Giovanni Vasanzio.

Pope Damasus wrote a remarkable poem for the martyr Eutychius, buried in the catacombs (the only one of his inscriptions to survive complete). Also remarkable are the carved wooden ceiling, the altar with the urn containing the remains of St. Sebastian and the statue of the saint, the Chapel of the Relics, containing one of the

arrows that pierced him, the column where he was tied up and the stone bearing the footprint believed to be Jesus' as recounted in the *Quo Vadis*, and, lastly, the Albani Chapel, designed by Carlo Fontana, with decorations dedicated to the martyred Pope St. Fabian (236–250).

THE CHURCH OF QUO VADIS

Situated between the Via Appia and the Via Ardeatina, refers to a famous episode in the story of St. Peter's captivity. Having been persuaded by zealous followers in the community to leave Rome and escape martyrdom, Peter was about to cross the gate when, in the exact place where the present church stands, Christ appeared to him. The Apostle was surprised, and asked: "Domine, quo vadis?" (Where are you going, Lord?). And the Lord replied: "I am going to Rome to be crucified for the second time." St. Peter understood, and so he went back to Rome to face his martyrdom. The church contains a copy of the stone bearing the Lord's footprint (the original is in the basilica of San Sebastiano fuori le Mura).

PRACTICAL INFORMATION

Via Appia Antica, 136.
☎ 06 785 03 50.
🚌 118, 218.
Closed: Sunday, mid-November to mid-December.
www.catacombe.org

The original basilica was dedicated by Constantine to Peter and Paul. All that is left of it is the outer nave: the long spaces to the right and to the left of the present basilica. The former is used as a ticket office for the catacombs, and houses a rich collection

The crypt of San Sebastiano was connected to the church by two staircases, still visible today.

of local sarcophagi. The portion on the left is partly used as an exit from the catacombs, partly as church sacristy and partly as a museum of inscriptions with an interesting scale model of the various phases of construction. There once were huge mausoleums adjacent to Constantine's basilica, among them the so-called "Platonia," built in the 4th century by the Pannonians (Hungarians) living in Rome, in which the martyr Quirinus, Bishop of the Pannonian city of Siscia, was buried. The catacombs have always been open. Among those who spent hours there in prayer were St. Bridget of Sweden and her daughter St. Catherine, St. Philip Neri (who included them in the pilgrimage of the Seven Churches), St. Pius V and St. Charles Borromeo. The crypt where St. Sebastian is buried, with a bust of the saint attributed to Bernini, and the *cubiculum* of St. Philip Neri are both worth visiting.

The *triclia* is a space enclosed by a portico, originally open, where Christians would venerate Peter and Paul or their relics. The hundreds of scratched supplications addressed to the two Apostles testify to the ritual banquets (*refrigerium*) that took place in their memory. The reason why this devotion took place on the Via Appia was probably because the martyrs could not be venerated at their respective tombs in the Vatican and on the Via Ostiense due to the violent persecution of Christians by the Emperor Valerian in the second half of the 3rd century. Later, Constantine had the basilica built on the site. Below the *triclia* was a piece of land with three

mausoleums (of *Clodius Hermes*, of the *Innocentiores*, and of the *Ascia*), magnificent pagan structures with painted and stucco decorations. Inscriptions and paintings of New Testament subjects confirm that, from the 3rd century, Christians were also buried there. To the west of the mausoleums are the large and small villas, both dating from pagan times. The oldest and deepest area (12 meters below the basilica) reveals pagan *columbaria* (chambers with wall niches to hold the urns containing the ashes), and poor burials in the pozzolana quarry.

The small villa is decorated with frescoes framed by narrow red and green lines (first decades of the third century). It was probably the seat of a funerary committee, whose task was to ensure that its members received proper burial.

The model shows the unique structure of the basilica of Constantine, with its elliptical plan reminiscent of that of Roman circuses. Constantine ordered many basilicas to be built in this style close to important sanctuaries in the outskirts of Rome.

Catacombs of Domitilla

The catacombs of Domitilla extend along the old Via Ardeatina. They grew out of clusters of underground burial chambers, some of them belonging to pagan families who then joined the Christian community. As the number of burials increased, the catacombs joined up, forming a single huge network, with over 12 kilometers of galleries. They are the largest in Rome, so large that Antonio Bosio almost lost his way in them. Nereus and Achilleus are the most important martyrs venerated here. They were both soldiers, perhaps praetorian guards, who were probably victims of the terrible persecutions of Diocletian.

Another martyr mentioned in the sources, but whose true history is a matter of debate, is Petronilla. She is the subject of an entirely uncorroborated story that she was St. Peter's daughter, perhaps because of the similarity of their names. Petronilla was known as the "succour of the Frankish nation," and for that reason her remains were moved to the chapel of the Frankish Kings in the Vatican, later destroyed to make way for the present St. Peter's basilica, during the time of Paul I (757–767). In the early Middle Ages, the cemetery fell into a state of serious neglect and was unsafe, as Pope Gregory the Great himself complained in a memorable sermon. For that reason, the cult of the two martyrs gradually moved to the very ancient parish church near the Baths of Caracalla (the fourth-century "parish church of Fasciola").

The catacombs are arranged on two levels. Their size makes it impossible to visit the whole cemetery, but the visitor can follow a set route through part of it. Starting at the entrance, we come to:

1) The basilica of Santi Neree e Achilleo. The present building dates from the end of the 4th century, in the papacy of Siricius (384–399), who continued his predecessor Damasus' veneration of the martyrs. It was built on top of a private burial chamber in which the two martyrs had been laid. Petronilla must also have been buried near them. The building, which is half underground, is of considerable grandeur. It was abandoned in the 9th century, and rediscovered following excavations by de Rossi in 1874. A narthex stands in front of the body of the church, which has an apse. The interior is divided into three naves by columns whose capitals have been taken from elsewhere. The upper part of the church and the roof were reconstructed after it was discovered. The burial place of Nereus and Achilleus corresponded to the present altar. Remains of the early medieval *schola cantorum* can be seen. The church contains a collection

PRACTICAL INFORMATION

Via delle Sette Chiese, 282.

06 511 03 42.

218, 716.

Closed: Tuesday, the month of January, Easter, Dec. 25.

The cubiculum of Diogenes the digger is a fourth-century crypt, perhaps occupied by the leader of the workmen who excavated the catacombs. The picture shows the damage caused in the 18th century by efforts to remove the frescoes.

the 3rd century, Christians were buried there, and decoration inspired by Scripture was added. De Rossi believed that members of the family of the Flavii, Christian members of the nobility and relatives of Domitilla, may have been buried there, but there is no evidence for this. The external façade of the chamber, a well and an area for the ritual of the funeral feast, as well as seats for banquets, have all survived. The cubiculum of Cupid and Psyche, elegantly painted, completes the complex.

4) The so-called "great stair" area of Tor Marancia is very ancient, and was deepened several times. Of note are the *cubiculum* of the Good Shepherd, with paintings from the mid-3rd century, and the *cubiculum* of David.

5) Another ancient and once separate burial is called the *cubiculum* of Ampliatus, from its owner's name, carved on a large marble tablet. Especially of interest are the loftier, arched tombs of the Minor Apostles, the *cubiculum* of Diogenes the digger, of interest because its frescoes show the tools used by the workmen who excavated the catacombs, the cubiculum of Orpheus, the Crypt of the Six Saints and the Crypt of the Bakers, the painting of the Madonna with four Magi and the arched tomb with a mosaic of Christ between Peter and Paul.

of sarcophagi and inscriptions excavated in the surrounding area.

2) Near the basilica is a cubiculum with a wonderful late-fourth-century painting of St. Petronilla, leading the deceased Veneranda into Paradise.

3) One of the oldest clusters is the burial chamber of the Flavii, initiated at the end of the second century for private pagan burials, with large niches for sarcophagi and fine naturalistic painting. During

THE CATACOMBS OF DOMITILLA

They were named for the noblewoman Flavia Domitilla, the niece of Flavius Clemens, Consul in 95 AD, who had married the daughter of one of Emperor Domitian's sisters (Domitian was Emperor from 81 to 96), also called Flavia Domitilla. This branch of the Flavian dynasty seems to have had Christian sympathies as pagan historians speak of punishments inflicted for religious reasons on the Consul and his wife: he was sentenced to death, and she was exiled to the island of Ventotene. But the Christian historian Eusebius tells us that Flavia Domitilla, the Consul's niece, was sentenced by Domitian to be deported to the island of Ponza with other Roman matrons, because she was a Christian.

The underground chamber of the Flavii Flavia Domitilla, before her exile, had made available to the Christian communities her earthly goods on the Via Ardeatina, which is where the catacomb would be located.

Catacombs of Priscilla

Priscilla must have been the founder of the cemetery, or perhaps the donor of the land on which it was built. As a surviving funerary inscription shows, Priscilla was related to the aristocratic family of the Acilii, mentioned by the historians Suetonius and Dio Cassius, who record that a certain Acilius Glabrio, Consul in 91 AD, was sentenced to death by Domitian, along with members of other senatorial families, probably for adhering to the Christian faith. These historical sources locate the burial places of many martyrs and Popes in Priscilla's catacombs. Among the most famous recorded are the brothers Felix and Philip, sons of St. Felicitas, martyred in 304 in the Diocletianic persecutions, with their five other brothers: Alexander, Martial, Vitalis, Sylvanus and Januarius. Among Popes, they mention Marcellinus (296–304), Marcellus (308–309), Sylvester (314–335), Liberius (352–366), Siricius (384–399), Celestine (422–432) and Vigilius (537–555). This makes it the third most important papal cemetery, after the Vatican Grottos and the catacombs of San Callisto. The catacombs, situated on the ancient Via Salaria Nova (so called because it was used to bring salt to Rome from the Adriatic), are one of the largest. They are constructed on two levels, the upper, and older, being irregular and unplanned, while the lower is very orderly, with large parallel galleries, branching at right angles. The upper level can be visited, and includes:

1) The *cubiculum* of the Veiled Woman, with paintings of the second half of the 3rd century, representing salient moments from the life of a young woman, clearly the one buried in the *cubiculum:* marriage, motherhood and death.

2) The niche of the Madonna and Child with the prophet Balaam, indicated by a star (see Numbers 24:17). The tenderness with which Mary is depicted holding the child close to her is particularly worth noting. Some people believe it is not Balaam but another prophet (Isaiah, Micah or David) who is represented, on the basis of other relevant biblical references.

3) The central area of the Arenario consists of a series of galleries originally dug out in order to extract the typical Roman pozzolana earth,

PRACTICAL INFORMATION

Via Salaria 430.
☎ FAX 06 86 20 62 72.
🚌 63, 86, 92, 310.
Closed: Monday, month of January.
www.catacombepriscilla.com

The cryptoporticus was used as a burial place by a patrician family, and later connected to the catacombs. It houses the very precious Greek Chapel.

used to make the best quality building cement. About the first quarter of the 3rd century, the Christian community re-used these galleries as a burial place for poor people, saving labor since they had already been excavated. The simple inscriptions in red lead on the slabs that close the burial recesses are of particular interest.

4) The cryptoporticus and Greek Chapel. This is an underground space, with masonry walls, originally the burial place of a high-ranking family, and only later linked to the catacombs. The Greek Chapel, so called because it contains Greek inscriptions, is important for its late third-century frescoes. They show unusual scenes, including a cycle of the trial of Susanna, a eucharistic banquet and the phoenix in the flames, a pagan emblem adopted by the Christians; there was an ancient belief that this bird could rise from its own ashes.

5) The burial place of the Acilii. This was originally a large water tank belonging to a cemetery at ground level, and was later used for Christian burials. Inscriptions of the noble Acilii family, relatives of Priscilla, were found here.

6) The basilica of Pope St. Sylvester is outside the catacombs, in the present Villa Ada. At the beginning of the 4th century, Pope Sylvester had a basilica built in the cemetery above the ground, whose altar was in the same position as the tomb of the martyrs Felix and Philip. Sylvester himself and Pope Siriacus were buried there.

WOMEN IN THE EARLY CHRISTIAN COMMUNITY

Women played a very important role in the earliest Christian community, as it was thanks to the generosity of noblewomen that the Church could find the human and material resources it required to meet the needs of the poor and the community. Some of the names of these generous benefactresses were: Prisca, Lucina, Priscilla, Domitilla, Commodilla, Generosa and Octavilla, and so on. They made available houses and land the community could use to build churches and cemeteries. Nonetheless, many of them, in Africa, Spain, Sicily and Asia Minor, as well as Rome, paid by martyrdom for professing the new faith. The most famous Roman women martyrs are: St. Agnes, St. Emerentiana, St. Cecilia, St. Felicitas (who gave her life with her seven sons, Sylvanus, Vitalis, Martial, Alexander, Felix, Philip and Januarius), St. Bassilla, St. Beatrice, St. Eugenia, St. Thecla and St. Petronilla.

The galleries of the Arenario, originally excavated in order to extract a type of earth called pozzolana, were used by the Christians as burial places.

A view of the Greek Chapel, which was recently restored. In the foreground, the cycle of frescoes of Susanna.

Catacombs of Sant'Agnese

These catacombs take their name from Agnes, the celebrated Roman martyr, who was buried there and who, we can be fairly sure, was a victim of the bloody persecutions of Diocletian. Many authors in antiquity wrote about her: Ambrose, Damasus and Prudentius, were fascinated by this heroic young girl.

However, it is uncertain whether Ambrose wrote the well-known hymn about her. These texts tell us that Agnes was only twelve when she died, but there is great uncertainty about how she was put to death. Damasus speaks of her being burned at the stake, Ambrose and Prudentius of beheading, while the hymn says that the veins of her neck were cut. Prudentius refers to a detail of the torture Agnes endured, which would be frequently exploited in later legendary stories about the saint: she was exposed naked in a brothel, in a vault of the stadium of Domitian, on the site of the present Piazza Navona. In the early Middle Ages there was in fact a small chapel there dedicated to her, and later replaced by the large seventeenth-century church of Francesco Borromini, Sant'Agnese in Agone.

The young martyr's body was then laid in a burial chamber belonging to her family, on the left of the Via Nomentana, at what is known today as Porta Pia. The cemetery, which became a communal one, was soon named after her.

From the beginning, Agnes's young age and amazing strength of mind inspired deep devotion among both Romans and foreigners. She was greatly venerated, even by the family of the Emperor Constantine. In fact, on this site was built one of the typical elliptical churches of the Constantinian period, with an awe-inspiring round mausoleum, known as the Mausoleum of Santa

PRACTICAL INFORMATION

Via Nomentana, 349.

☎ 06 86 10 54 840.

🚌 36, 60, 84, 90, 136, 137.

Opening hours: 9 a.m.–12 p.m., 4–6 p.m.

Closed: Sunday (and holidays), and from Oct. 23–Nov. 23.

www.santagnese.com

Costanza, where the Emperor's daughter Constantia was buried. In the time of Pope Symmachus (498–514) a small basilica was built, directly above Agnes's tomb. Pope Honorius (625–638) built on the burial site the present monumental, half-underground basilica of Sant'Agnese.

A tour of this sanctuary is fairly complicated but of great interest, because of the number and importance of archaeological finds. Going underground from the outside the following can be admired:

CONSTANTIA, DAUGHTER OF CONSTANTINE

The Emperor Constantine had five children by his wife Fausta: Constantine II, Constantius II, Constans, Constantia and Helena, the future wife of Julian the Apostate. After her conversion, Constantia married her father's half-brother Hannibalianus, King of Pontus and Cappadocia. She died in Bithynia in 354, and her body was brought back to Rome in 360 and placed in the mausoleum that she herself had had built next to the great elliptical basilica dedicated to St. Agnes. Her sister Helena was also buried in the mausoleum.

St. Agnes, martyred at the age of twelve, was greatly venerated after her death by both Romans and foreigners. (The picture shows St. Agnese praying, marble slab, detail.)

The remains of the Constantinian Basilica and, to the right, the Mausoleum.

The Mausoleum of Santa Costanza, characterized by a circular plan, was built in the fourth century. The dome and drum are supported by arches resting on twelve pairs of granite columns.

was buried), was erected beside the church.

The interior was divided into two concentric parts, separated by a double granite colonnade. The outer part had eleven niches, in one of which was placed Constantia's magnificent porphyry sarcophagus. It is preserved, with the similar one belonging to Helena, in the Vatican Museums, and a copy has been placed in the mausoleum.

The ceilings were covered in mosaics that portrayed cupids harvesting grapes; those of the dome have been destroyed, but those of the outer circle (the ambulatory) and of the two niches are wonderfully preserved.

1) The elliptical Constantinian basilica: unfortunately these buildings were not durable, and were all destroyed or only partially survive, except for the above-mentioned San Sebastiano. Only the walls of the basilica, including the curve of the apse, remain, pierced by windows. It was built thanks to the good offices, and at the expense, of Constantina or Constantia, daughter of the Emperor Constantine, who had converted to Christianity and whom later legends turned into a saint; hence the name Santa Costanza.

2) The Mausoleum of Santa Costanza. Constantia was so devoted to St. Agnes that in addition to building a basilica, she also wanted to be buried near her tomb. So the extraordinary circular mausoleum, with a roof and a dome (like that of Santi Marcellino e Peter, where Constantine's mother Helena

3) The basilica of Honorius: this was built by Pope Honorius I above the tomb of St. Agnes, replacing the little church of Pope Symmachus, which was in ruins. It is half underground, reached by a stair on which is inscribed the solemn poem of Damasus to St. Agnes. The

THE BLESSING OF THE LAMBS

On January 21, the feast of the Roman Virgin, two white lambs are blessed on the altar of Sant'Agnese by the Abbot General of the Lateran Canons Regular. Lying comfortably in a basket, the lambs each wear a crown of red roses (martyrdom) and white roses (purity). Their wool will later be used by the cloistered Benedictine nuns of the convent of Santa Cecilia in Trastevere to make the holy *pallia* (a *pallium* is a narrow stole), part of the vestments worn only by the Pope and metropolitan Bishops. This tradition began in the 16th century and continues today, and it has a very specific meaning. By wearing the *pallia*, the Bishops clothes themselves in the heroic virtues of St. Agnes: faith, strength and purity.

The mosaics of the Mausoleum of Santa Costanza feature flowers, fruit, birds and scenes of country life.

interior, preceded by a narthex, has three naves, divided by columns with fine Corinthian capitals. There is an internal gallery above the side naves. The mosaic in the hemicircle of the apse is an outstanding example of Byzantine art, and shows Agnes between Pope Honorius and, probably, Pope Symmachus. Preserved in the high altar are some of the relics of St. Agnes and St. Emerentiana, another young martyr buried on the Via Nomentana, in the Coemeterium Maius.

4) The catacombs: these are on several levels, and their appearance shows the ravages of the so-called "holy body-snatchers," who ransacked the cells of the catacombs in the 17th and 18th centuries, hoping to take from them their "saintly bodies," which were often actually those of ordinary people, and exploit them commercially. The catacombs consist of four sections. The first, on the left-hand side of the Honorian basilica, is where St. Agnes's tomb was located. It has some very ancient features, such as its simple inscriptions. The other sections are all from the Constantinian era. The fourth, in particular, was excavated below the atrium of the Constantinian basilica, where there had been a pagan burial consisting of ten mausoleums from the end of the second century AD, destroyed to construct the basilica.

The Honorian basilica, which retains the form and structure of the fourth-century basilica, boasts splendid mosaics in the apse, one of which represents the Saint between two Popes.

Basilica and Catacombs of San Pancrazio

Near Villa Pamphili, on the Via Vitellia, which corresponds to a branch of the old Via Aurelia, stands the stunning basilica of San Pancrazio, which dates from the time of Pope Honorius I (625–638), though with many later modifications.

The church was built on the spot where the martyr Pancras was buried.

The traditions in regard to this martyr are somewhat confused and contradictory. It seems that the young Pancras, an orphan, came to Rome from Phrygia, converted to Christianity and, after suffering hardships, fell victim to the persecutions of Diocletian.

His body, abandoned on the Via Aurelia, was retrieved by the pious matron Octavilla and buried in a nearby cemetery. After his martyrdom this saint became the object of fervent popular devotion.

St. Gregory of Tours (538–594) and Pope St. Gregory the Great (590–604) both wrote about him. He was considered the protector of those accused of swearing false oaths. Moreover, there was a belief that perjurers would drop dead, or suffer demonic possession, if they went near his venerated tomb.

The catacombs of St. Pancras, also called the catacombs of Ottavilla, never fell into oblivion, and like those of St. Sebastian, St. Lawrence and St. Agnes, they have always been visited by pilgrims.

THE SEPULCHRE OF A MARTYR

The basilica of San Lorenzo fuori le Mura (*see p. 120*) holds a special place among the martyrs' sanctuaries. It was built above the martyr's tomb in a crypt within the catacomb of Cyriaca, in the Verano area, on the Via Tiburtina.

This was a problem for their physical preservation, and now only a small part is open to visitors. Some of the areas are notable for their decoration, such as the *cubicula* of Botrys, St. Felix and St. Sophia, and the area below the left transept of the church, where the saint's tomb was located, is interesting.

The first monument was constructed there in the time of Pope Symmachus (498–514), who built a small church above the venerated tomb.

The church was completely rebuilt under Honorius I (625–638). It was large, with three naves and a transept, an apse, a semicircular crypt (the oldest of this type after St. Peter's) and a raised sanctuary. This church was refurbished in the Middle Ages, with new Cosmatesque

PRACTICAL INFORMATION

Piazza San Pancrazio, 5/d.

C 06 58 10 458.

44, 75, 870, 871, 984.

Temporarily closed for restoration. For special permission to visit contact the Pontificia Commissione per l'Archeologica sacra (tel.: 06 44 65 610).

ornamentation, and further work was carried out under Cardinal Ludovico de Torres in 1609. Inside, apart from the crypt, the following features are of interest: the wooden ceiling, the stucco decoration of the naves, the frescoes in the sanctuary, attributed to Antonio Tempesta, and in the left-hand chapel, a painting of *St. Teresa of Avila* by Jacopo Palma the Younger, of 1615.

The façade as it looks today dates back to the late 5th century, during the papacy of Innocent VIII Cybo (1484–1492). Two columns support the tympanum of the central doorway, surmounted by the Cybo family's coat of arms.

The basilica of San Pancrazio, in an old print. For centuries the destiny of pilgrims and a place of worship, it was frequently ransacked by barbarian invaders.

Catacombs of Santi Marcellino e Pietro

Located on the old Via Labicana, now the Via Casilina, near the modern church of the same name, these catacombs were built in what was the heart of the great Imperial property *ad duas lauros* ("at the two laurels"), which extended from the Porta Maggiore, in the Aurelian Walls, as far as Rome's most easterly suburb. In the late 2nd century AD, before the Christian cemetery existed, this was the burial ground of the *Equites singulares Augusti*, the Emperor's horse guards, a select body many of whose gravestones have been found, reused as building material; from the middle of the 3rd century, Christians began to excavate galleries beneath it, to bury their dead. As in the other great catacombs, they first dug separate clusters of burial chambers which gradually expanded to form a vast cemetery, used by residents of one of the most densely populated parts of Rome, Subura. When the tombs of a number of martyrs were placed there, it brought a great expansion of the cemetery. They included Peter the exorcist and Marcellinus, a priest, both victims of Diocletian, buried in a crypt in the catacombs, Tiburtius, whose mausoleum is above ground, Gorgonius, buried in the catacombs,

but whose tomb has not been identified, and the Crowned Martyrs, saints from Pannonia who were venerated, perhaps in the form of relics, in a crypt in the cemetery, before being transferred to the church of the Santi Quattro Coronati in the city.

After his victory at the Milvian Bridge in 312, the Emperor Constantine had the site completely transformed. He had the cemetery of the *Equites singulares* destroyed and added some wonderful buildings to the sanctuary, including a large elliptical basilica, a circular mausoleum and two enclosures to either side of the basilica, containing many private mausoleums. Of all Constantine's work all that remain are the ruins of the domed mausoleum. These were originally

The fresco (at the turn of the fourth and fifth centuries) in the catacombs represents Christ between Sts. Peter and Paul, and below, the principal martyrs venerated *ad duas lauros*: St. Peter, St. Marcellinus, St. Tiburtius and St. Gorgonius.

covered in sumptuous marble and mosaic, in the same style as those in Santa Costanza. In a niche in the mausoleum there was a magnificent red porphyry sarcophagus, now in the Vatican Museums, containing the remains of the Emperor's mother Augusta Helena. In the 17th century, a small church with a presbytery was built inside the mausoleum, which will eventually be turned into a museum for the site.

Thanks to Constantine's many building projects, the cemetery became one of the most interested in the outskirts of Rome.

Pope Damasus was also involved in making it beautiful, embellishing the venerated tombs and giving them his distinctive verse inscriptions. The catacombs boast an exceptional wealth of paintings, with frescoes in over 85 rooms depicting lively, fresh scenes of both pagan and Christian inspiration. Among them should be mentioned the pictures of the diggers, the workers who excavated the cemetery, and the banqueting scenes. These are probably reproductions of family gatherings connected with the very ancient ritual of the *refrigerium*, which was performed in memory of a deceased relative on the anniversary of the day of his or her death.

Funeral banquet, part of the rite of the refrigerium, in the catacombs of Santi Marcellino e Pietro.

The Chapel of Santi Marcellino e Pietro, which at one time led to the catacombs, was built at the behest of Urban VIII Barberini in 1638.

SANTA PUDENZIANA

The basilica of Santa Pudenziana is located between the Esquiline and Viminal hills, lower down than the present level of Via Urbana and near Santa Maria Maggiore; according to late hagiographic tradition, the basilica is dedicated to one of two daughters of the senator Pudens.

The basilica was a *titulus*, what is referred to as a parish church today, built above a 2nd-century Roman house with heated baths, which some believe was a place of worship (*domus*

PRACTICAL INFORMATION

Via Urbana, 160.
 06 481 46 22.
 16, 75, 84, 105, 714.
 B Cavour.
Opening hours: 9 a.m.–12 p.m., 3 p.m.–6 p.m.

Funerary monument

Frieze on the architrave of the portico

The entrance doorway is supported by two columns. The frieze on the architrave was part of the 11th-century door.

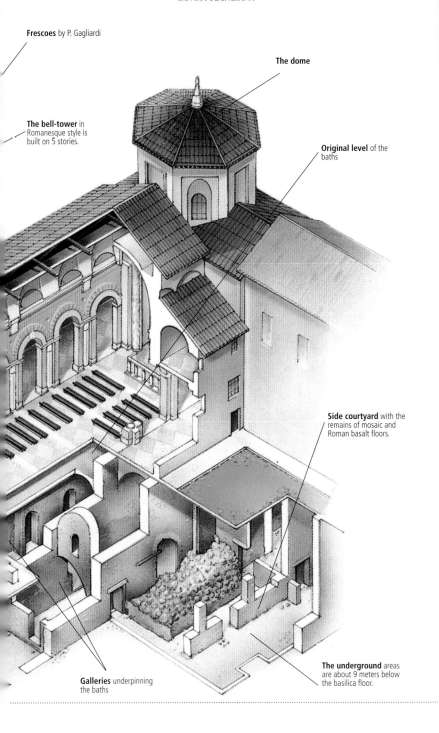

Frescoes by P. Gagliardi

The dome

The bell-tower in Romanesque style is built on 5 stories.

Original level of the baths

Side courtyard with the remains of mosaic and Roman basalt floors.

The underground areas are about 9 meters below the basilica floor.

Galleries underpinning the baths

ecclesiae) before the time of Constantine, but without conclusive evidence.

Built in the late 4th or early 5th century, featuring three naves with six columns on each side, the church was extensively altered, particularly at the turn of the sixteenth century by Francesco da Volterra. It became a single nave covered by a dome in the area of the sanctuary. The stunning mosaic in the apse survives from the early period; though heavily restored and reconstructed it is one of the earliest in existence.

It is a very large composition, still in the classical tradition, showing Christ enthroned and blessing, surrounded by the college of the Apostles and, probably, allegorical figures of the Churches of the Gentiles and the Hebrews (others think they represent St. Pudentiana and St. Praxedes), crowning Peter and Paul.

A cross decorated with jewels, symbolizing triumph, stands out in the background, placed at the summit of a hill, Golgotha, as does the monumental architecture of the celestial Jerusalem, with the symbols of the four Evangelists. The composition is framed in a background of nuanced clouds. The mosaic presents the Lord Jesus as the center and the joy of the Celestial Jerusalem. The Church of Christ, which marches joyfully towards Jerusalem, is represented by the house of Pudentiana, who gathers the assembly of the faithful. The scroll that Jesus holds in his left hand says that He, the Saviour, is their "Preserver."

The right-hand side of the mosaic is largely a reconstruction of the original, while the lower section is lost. It showed the mystical Lamb and the dove of the Holy Spirit, and a mosaic inscription recording the names of the donors: Ilicius, Maximus and Leopardus.

The present Caetani Chapel is a radical transformation of an existing early Christian oratory, dedicated to St. Pastor. The fine Romanesque bell-tower is from the early 13th century, and the doorway was made in the 16th century, using medieval materials.

Mosaic in the apse (detail), the earliest surviving example from a place of worship.

Bernardino Nocchi, *Glory of St. Pudenziana*, 1803–1806.

SAN CLEMENTE

The festive mosaic in the apse of the basilica of San Clemente, executed under Pope Paschal II in the first half of the 12th century, has a complex symbolic meaning, which is also related to the large motif of acanthus branches, a reference to the Resurrection. The central theme is the *Triumph of the Cross* on whose arms, next to Christ, are twelve doves representing the Apostles, between Mary and St. John. Acanthus scrolls grow naturally from the cross, framing a lively scene filled with small figures, both human and animal, while, lower down, two stags drink from the rivers of Paradise. The apsidal arch, in addition to the allegorical cities of Jerusalem and Bethlehem, depicts Christ with the symbols of the Evangelists, St. Peter and St. Clement, with the prophet Jeremiah, on one side, and St. Lawrence, St. Paul and the prophet Isaiah on the other. Underneath this, the early Christian motif of the Lamb of God appears again, surrounded by the twelve sheep, another symbol of the Apostles.

The church one enters today from Via San Giovanni in Laterano is the medieval one, with three naves ending in three apses, preceded by a four-sided portico; but the earlier phases of building at San Clemente are still visible. These include: the early Christian church, larger than the later one, a Mithraic temple, and the remains of ancient Roman buildings. All these building phases form a series of layers, which archaeological research carried out from the 19th century onwards has made coherent and accessible. Starting from the lowest level, the site was occupied by a public building dating from the 1st century AD, and later by a set of domestic buildings, whose courtyard was turned into a place of worship by the followers of the Persian god Mithras.

The early Christian basilica was built in the 4th century. It enjoyed the status of parish church (*titulus*), had three naves and a narthex. The earlier structures are difficult to distinguish because of the massive foundations

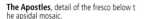

PRACTICAL INFORMATION

Via di San Giovanni in Laterano.

06 77 40 021.

85, 87, 117, 186, 810, 850.

B Colosseo.

Opening hours: 9 a.m.–12.30 p.m.; 3–6 p.m. Monday to Saturday; 12–6 p.m. on Sunday.

The Apostles, detail of the fresco below the apsidal mosaic.

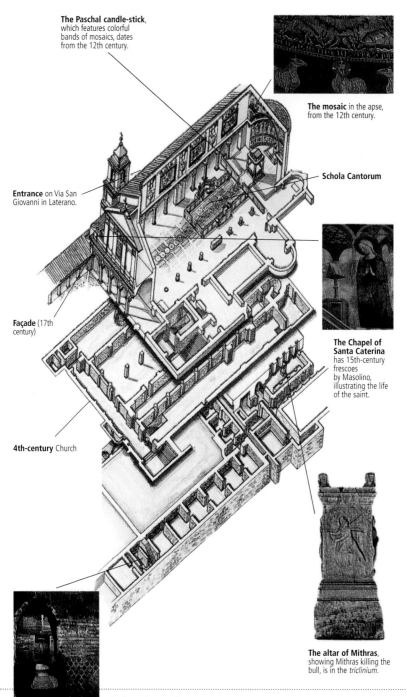

The Paschal candle-stick, which features colorful bands of mosaics, dates from the 12th century.

The mosaic in the apse, from the 12th century.

Schola Cantorum

Entrance on Via San Giovanni in Laterano.

Façade (17th century)

The Chapel of Santa Caterina has 15th-century frescoes by Masolino, illustrating the life of the saint.

4th-century Church

The altar of Mithras, showing Mithras killing the bull, is in the *triclinium*.

In the underground area, a 5th- or 6th-century cemetery containing 16 niches was discovered in 1938.

supporting the medieval church above.

Recent excavations have identified the baptistery attached to the early church.

Important frescoes have survived from the time of Pope Leo IV (847–855) and from the 11th and 12th centuries. They include the paintings of the *Legend of St. Alexis* and the *Legend of Sisinnius*. Also venerated is the tomb of St. Cyril, who, with St. Methodius, was one of those who took the Gospel to Eastern Europe. He invented the Cyrillic alphabet, which is still used in Russia today. In the upper church, the Chapel of Santa Caterina contains a cycle of marvelous frescoes by Masolino da Panicale, which were completed, perhaps in collaboration with Masaccio, between 1428 and 1431. The subjects depicted include the Crucifixion and episodes from the lives of St. Ambrose and St. Catherine of Alexandria.

CHRONOLOGY

2nd century Possibly a place of worship for Christians	**End of 2nd century** Building of the temple of Mithras	**867** St. Clement's remains are moved to Rome	**1108** New church built on the original 4th-century one	**1857** Father Mullooly discovered the original 4th-century church	

10 AD	500	1000	1500	1900

90–99 Papacy of St. Clement	**4th century** First church built on the courtyard of the previous Roman buildings	**1084** Church destroyed during the Norman invasion guided by Robert Guiscard	**1667** Church and convent handed over to Irish Dominicans	**1861** Roman ruins are discovered

Masolino da Panicale, *Story of St. Ambrose*, 1428–1431, Branda Castiglioni Chapel

The Schola Cantorum, (choir), dating from the 6th century, was preserved in the new church built in 1108.

The atrium with a four-sided portico, leading
to the basilica.

❶ SANTA MARIA IN ARACOELI

Piazza d'Aracoeli
☎ 06 69 76 38 39
🚌 40, 62, 63, 64, 95, 170
Ⓜ Colosseo
Opening hours: 9 a.m.–12:30 p.m.; winter: 9:30 a.m.–12:30 p.m., 2:30–6:30 p.m.

The church was probably built in the 6th century, on the northern side of the Capitol hill, on the site of the temple of Juno. It is preceded by a wide staircase made up of 124 steps, completed in 1348 under Cola di Rienzo. The name *Aracoeli*, which means altar of heavens, derives from a 4th-century legend that the Virgin appeared to Augustus. The present Franciscan church dates from the late 13th century. Changes to the interior carried out in the latter part of the 16th century meant that the apse with its frescoes by Pietro Cavallini had

to be sacrificed. The present façade is dated to the 1200s, but the three doors were made later. The interior is divided into three naves by 22 columns salvaged from other buildings, and a wooden ceiling commemorating the battle of Lepanto (1571) with *Mary and the Child* in the center. The sanctuary contains a 10th- or 11th-century icon of the Madonna and Child which was venerated during the plague of 1348. In the transept on the left, the Chapel of Sant'Elena has a Cosmatesque altar and a 12th-century figure of Mary appearing to the kneeling Augustus. A copy of the 15th-century statue in olive wood from the Garden of Gethsemane is visible in the Chapel of the Holy Child. The fresco of the *Madonna and Child Enthroned between Sts. Matthew and John* is also attributed to Pietro Cavallino.

❷ SANTA MARIA IN CAMPITELLI

Piazza Campitelli, 9
☎ 06 68 80 39 78
🚌 40, 46, 62, 63, 64, 70, 87, 186, 780, 810
Ⓜ Colosseo, Circo Massimo
Opening hours: 7:30 a.m.–12:30 p.m., 3:30–7 p.m.

Located not far from Largo Argentina is the church of Santa Maria in Campitelli which contains a venerated image of Mary. The church was rebuilt by Carlo Rainaldi in Late Baroque style in the first half of the 17th century. The high altar preserves the 11th-century icon, made of silver leaf and enamel, called *Santa Maria in Portico, Romanus portus securitas*. It is believed to have saved Rome from an epidemic in 1656.

❸ Santa Maria della Consolazione

Piazza della Consolazione, 84
☎ 06 67 84 654
🚌 23, 44, 63, 81, 95, 160, 170, 280, 628, 715, 716, 780
Ⓜ Colosseo, Circo Massimo
Opening hours: 6:30 a.m.–6 p.m.

The church of Santa Maria della Consolazione was at one time attached to the hospital of the same name (built in 1470, destroyed in 1936) on the Vico Jugario on the slopes of the Capitol hill. It was rebuilt by Martino Longhi the Elder towards the end of the 16th century. The church has three naves with side chapels, and it contains many valuable works with Mary as their theme. Located above the high altar is a venerated fresco depicting the *Virgin of Consolation*, executed during the Middle Ages, but reworked by Antoniazzo Romano (late 15th century). Beside it are Pomarancio's *Nativity* and *Assumption*; in the chapel to the right of the sanctuary is a 13th-century icon of the Virgin, and in the second chapel on the right a *Madonna and Child with Saints* by Livio Agresti (1575). Also of interest, in another chapel, are the frescoes of the *Passion* by Taddeo Zuccari (1556).

❹ Santi Cosma e Damiano

Via dei Fori Imperiali, 1
☎ 06 69 20 441
🚌 85, 87, 117, 175, 186, 810, 850
Ⓜ Colosseo, Circo Massimo
Opening hours: 9 a.m.–1 p.m., 3–7 p.m.

This church was built by Felix IV (526–530) over pre-existing classical structures, identified with the library of the Forum of Peace, and a chamber belonging to the temple of the Divine Romulus, on the "Via Sacra." The outer wall had cladding consisting of 150 marble slabs, making up the ancient Forma Urbis, i.e. the monumental plan of Rome at the time of the Severi. The church has remained largely unchanged since the first half of the 17th century, when the floor was raised by approximately 7 meters due to water seepage, and the interior was altered by sacrificing the far ends of the mosaics in the original apse. Its dedication to the doctor-saints relates to the spread of their cult, especially during the 6th century. In the center of

the vault of the apse, Christ soars in heaven, dressed in gold, under the hand of God, and between Peter and Paul, who present Cosmas and Damian. Next come St. Theodore and Pope Felix IV, the latter with a small model of the church in his hand; lower down is the *Agnus Dei* (Lamb of God) with twelve sheep symbolizing the Apostles. The triumphal arch, possibly executed under Pope Sergius I (692–701), depicts the Apocalypse, with the mystic Lamb carrying the Cross.

❺ SAN TEODORO

Via di San Teodoro, 7
☎ 06 67 86 624
🚌 23, 44, 81, 95, 160, 170, 280, 628, 715, 716
Ⓜ Colosseo, Circo Massimo
Opening hours: 9:30 a.m.–12:30 p.m., Sun–Fri

The earliest certain evidence that a charitable institution consisting of a church and a convent existed on this site is from the 9th century. Until the 16th century, the bronze she-wolf from the Capitol was preserved here. The name comes from the legendary Roman soldier from Asia Minor, who was sent to the stake for refusing to offer up a sacrifice, and for burning down a temple dedicated to the goddess Cybele, probably under the Emperor Diocletian in the 3rd century. His cult was widespread throughout the Greek and Latin Christian worlds. The church was nicknamed "Santo Toto," and mothers would take their sick children there to be healed. Like the Mausoleum of Santa Costanza and Santo Stefano Rotondo, it is on

a circular plan, and was restored under Nicholas V (1447–1455), as proven by the recently excavated ancient ruins and the 6th-century mosaic. Its present appearance is a transformation of the design by the architect Bernardo Rossellino; it was first renovated in 1643 on the orders of Cardinal Barberini, and later, in 1705, under Pope Clement XI, by the architect Carlo Fontana. In order to clear earth and water from the depression in the ground, Fontana designed the rectangular parvis in front of the church, accessible from street level by two curved converging staircases. He also added a chapel, the sacristy and a room for vestments. The church was handed over to the Society of the Sacred Heart of Jesus, also known as the "Confraternita dei Sacconi Rossi," which promotes devotion to the Sacred Heart and fights blasphemy. It is also known for its special Good Friday ceremony. Inside it are two side altars and a high altar, the latter with an old Russian icon of the Virgin and Child. In the apse is a 6th-century mosaic depicting the *Saviour between Sts. Peter, Paul, Theodore and Cleonicus.* The figure of St. Theodore, cloaked in a gold-spangled mantle, was added at the time of the restoration carried out under Nicholas V.

6 SAN GIORGIO IN VELABRO

Via del Velabro, 19
📞 06 69 20 45 34
🚌 23, 44,63, 81, 95, 160, 170, 280, 628, 715, 716, 780
Ⓜ Colosseo, Circo Massimo
Opening hours: 8:30 a.m–7 p.m.

The church was built, probably by Pope Leo II (682–683), on a marshy piece of land called the "Velabrum" where, according to the legend, the shepherd Faustulus rescued Remus and Romulus. It is not far from the Arco degli Argentari, dating from the times of the Severi, and it was originally dedicated to St. Sebastian. Pope Zacharias (741–752) ordered that the relics of St. George be moved there from the Lateran Palace. The building was part of an ancient charitable institution established by the Church to assist the Christian community in Rome. The five-story Romanesque bell-tower dates from the 13th century. The interior is divided into three irregular naves by salvaged columns with no bases. The fresco in the apse, representing *Christ, Mary and Sts. George, Peter and Sebastian*, is of the school of Cavallini, but heavily restored. In the raised sanctuary, the Cosmatesque altar is surmounted by a canopy with architrave, dating from the 12th or 13th century. On July 27, 1993, the church's 13th-century portico, the gift of Prior Stefano Stella, and the convent were damaged by a bomb.

7 SANT'ANASTASIA

Piazza di Sant'Anastasia
📞 06 67 82 980
🚌 81, 160, 170, 628, 810
Ⓜ Colosseo, Circo Massimo

A *titulus* since the 4th century, the church was later restored by several Popes: Damasus (366–384), Hilarius (461–468), John VII (706–707) and Gregory IV (827–844). Legend made Anastasia, who was martyred during Diocletian's persecutions and venerated in Constantinople, where her relics had been transferred, a Roman martyr. Her name was superimposed on that of the woman who founded the *titulus Anastasiae* of the ancient basilica. The present façade, built of brick with two stories of pilaster strips and twin bell-towers, was designed by Arrigucci for Urban VIII (1623–1644). In 1615 the altar of the Holy Cross was dedicated to the Confraternity of the Cross and St. Anastasia, a tailors' and coat-makers' guild. The interior was restored first in the early 18th century at the request of the Portuguese Cardinal Nuno da Cunha, and then again in the 19th century under Pius VII (1800–1823) and Pius IX (1846–1878). It is divided into three naves by six pillars, with the marble columns salvaged from the early basilica placed against them. The coffered wooden ceiling dates from the 18th century, and the 17th-century Chapel of the Relics contains paintings by Lazzaro Baldi representing episodes from the lives of St. Charles Borromeo and St. Philip Neri. In the area under the church are the ruins of a portico dating from the 1st century of the Empire and of a group of *insulae* (dwellings). Pope St. Leo the Great, during the Mass at dawn on Christmas morning, gave a homily against Eutyches, the theologian who put forward the heresy that denied Christ's human nature: ever since then Popes celebrate one of the three Christmas Masses at dawn at Sant'Anastasia.

❽ SANTA MARIA IN COSMEDIN

Piazza Bocca della Verità, 18
📞 06 67 81 415
🚌 23, 44, 81, 95, 160, 170, 280, 628, 715, 716
Ⓜ Colosseo, Circo Massimo
Opening hours: 9:30 a.m.–6 p.m.(winter 5 p.m.)

The *mascherone* (a grotesque mask) popularly known as the "Bocca della Verità" (mouth of truth) is situated on the left-hand side of the portico of this church. It is a Roman manhole cover, possibly from a well or a branch of the Cloaca Maxima, placed here in 1632 atop a Corinthian capital. The first reports of the existence of a *diaconia* (a church with a charitable building attached to it) date back to the 6th century, and refer to Santa Maria *in Schola Graeca*, because the Byzantine-Greek community made it its main church. The edifice was rebuilt in 782 by Pope Adrian I, and sheltered those exiled under the iconoclastic persecutions of Constantine V Copronymus (774–780). It seems that at the time it was called *Kosmidion* because of its sumptuous decoration. In the 9th century a sacristy and an oratory, dedicated to St. Nicholas, were added. The

complex was destroyed by Robert Guiscard (in 1082), and then restored by Pope Gelasius II (1118–1119). Later changes included a new façade on the portico, with a vestibule in the center, under Calixtus II (1119–1124), and the Romanesque seven-story bell-tower. In the 18th century the church took on a Baroque appearance, but was restored to its original style at the end of the 19th. It is divided into three naves, with pillars and salvaged columns, a pavement imitating Cosmatesque style (the portion in the *Schola Cantorum* is original), and a ceiling rebuilt in the late 18th century. The internal gallery, dating from the 8th century, but closed by Pope Calixtus II, was also renewed then. Roman structures, thought to belong to the residence of the Prefect in charge of food supplies, have been found under the church. The 12th-century Schola Cantorum, with two pulpits and an iconostasis, as well as the red granite altar, with its late 13th-century canopy by Deodato, son of Cosma the younger, occupy much of the central nave. The crypt, in three sections, was carved out of an enormous block of tufa, possibly from the great altar of Hercules. Since 1639, a mosaic of the *Adoration of the Magi*, from the destroyed oratory of Giovanni VII (706–707) in St. Peter's, has been displayed in the 17th-century sacristy, modified in the eighteenth century.

❾ SANTI GIOVANNI E PAOLO

Piazza dei Santi Giovanni e Paolo, 13
📞 06 70 45 45 44
🚌 75, 81, 117, 175, 673
Ⓜ Circo Massimo, Colosseo
Opening hours: 10 a.m.–1 p.m., 3–6 p.m., Mo–Fri

The church rises up on the remains of the house of the two officials of Constantine's court martyred by Julian the Apostate for adhering to the Christian faith and buried in their house in 361. The church was modified in the early 18th century, and in the late 19th century the remains of the saints' house were brought back to light. The façade is divided into a portico, with eight columns, and an upper part with five arches supported on ancient marble columns. The Romanesque bell-tower, whose six upper stories are decorated with ceramic discs in various colors, rests on a foundation of blocks of travertine marble, the remains of the Temple of Claudius. The seven arches on the left, 13th- and 14th-century buttresses, are supported by pieces of ancient Roman masonry. The interior, which features three naves, contains a fresco by Pomarancio (1588), *The Redeemer in Glory*, in the apse, and a porphyry basin at the high altar, with relics of the two saints. Located

⓫ SANTA SABINA

Piazza Pietro d'Illiria, 1
 06 57 94 06 00
 23, 280, 716
 Circo Massimo
Opening hours: 6:30
a.m.–12:45 p.m., 3–7 p.m.

(winter 6 p.m.)

underground are the remains of a pool, with 2nd- and 3rd-century frescoes, a pagan Roman house, an early Christian house (possibly that of the two saints) and an early medieval oratory. There is also a tiny room with 9th- and 12th-century frescoes representing the martyrdom of the two saints.

⓾ SANTO STEFANO ROTONDO

Via di Santo Stefano Rotondo, 7
 06 42 11 99
 Circo Massimo
 81, 673, 117
Visits by appointment, call 06 0608

This church rises up on the road that runs alongside the aqueduct of Nero, and dates from the time of Pope Simplicius I (468–483). Its mosaic and marble decoration was added between 523 and 530. It was built on a

circular plan (the earliest in Rome for a church), though its exterior was cruciform. It consisted of three concentric areas, with eight entrances and four radial chapels. The chapel of Sts. Primus and Felician, with a 7th-century decoration in the apse portraying Christ between the two martyrs, has survived.

This early Christian Roman basilica on the Aventine hill is almost intact, with its three naves and their columns, its broad windows, the mosaic with inscriptions in gold lettering on the inner façade and the allegorical figures of two women symbolizing the Churches of the Jews and the Gentiles, the two main components of the Christian community headed by Peter and Paul. Building was started in the first half of the 5th century under Pope Celestine I (422–432) and completed under Sixtus III (432–440). The original decoration of the apse was replaced by a 16th-century fresco by Taddeo Zuccari, but many of the panels of the wooden door, with the story of Moses and New Testament scenes, have survived. These include the first appearance in Christian iconography of the Crucifixion of Christ between the two thieves.

⑫ SANT'ALESSIO ALL'AVENTINO

Piazza Sant'Alessio, 23
📞 06 57 43 446
🚌 23, 280, 716
Ⓜ Circo Massimo, Piramide
Opening hours: 9–11:45 a.m., 3:30–6:30 p.m.

(winter 6 p.m.)

The church was dedicated to St. Boniface the Martyr in the 3rd or 4th century, it became a *diaconia* in the 8th, and later it was also dedicated to St. Alexis, by whose name it is known at present. The medieval building from the time of Pope Honorius III (1216–1227) was altered by order of Cardinal Querini in 1750. The Somaschi order, present since 1846, initiated other restoration works. Especially of interest are the bell-tower, the crypt, and Cosmatesque work including: the portal,

the floor and the small columns of the choir. In the transept (on the right) is a 13th-century Byzantine icon of the Virgin.

⑬ SAN SABA

Piazza Bernini, 20
📞 06 64 58 01 40
🚌 75, 175, 673
🚋 3
Ⓜ Circo Massimo, Piramide
Opening hours: 8:30 a.m.–12 p.m., 4–6:30 p.m., Mon–Sat; Sun 9:30 a.m.–1

p.m., 4–6:30 p.m.
In 645 a group of monks from the monastery of San Saba, in Palestine, settled in a domus on the little hill where the church would later be built. The antipope Constantine was held prisoner there in 768. The church first presents its vestibule, at the top of a flight of steps leading to a green courtyard overlooked by the façade. The original façade is hidden behind the portico and the 15th-century arcade. The interior consists of three naves divided by salvaged columns. The sanctuary is raised, with a crypt below it. Above its altar is a canopy supported on columns of black

marble. There is a series of frescoes in the hemicircle of the apse, painted for the Jubilee of 1575, which is a reproduction of an earlier mosaic. Preserved in the right-hand nave are the remains of Cosmatesque work by Vassalletto. In the small nave on the left, originally perhaps a portico, are frescoes from the late 11th or early 12th century, representing the Virgin, St. Andrew, St. Nicholas and St. Sabbas. In the corridor leading to the sacristy are the remains of 7th- or 8th-century frescoes portraying the monks of the Eastern community.

⑭ SAN PIETRO IN MONTORIO

Piazza San Pietro in Montorio, 2
📞 06 58 13 940
Ⓜ Circo Massimo
🚌 44, 75
Opening hours: 8:30–12 a.m., 3–6 p.m. (summer

4–6 p.m.), Mon–Fri

A chapel already existed on this site in the late 9th

century. In 1472 Sixtus V handed the church and convent over to the Spanish congregation of the Amadeites and they, with the help of the King and Queen of Spain, began to build a new church, designed by Baccio Pontelli and Meo del Caprino. The church has a single nave with frescoes by Sebastiano del Piombo (*The Flagellation*, *The Ascension* and *The Prophets,* dated to 1518), by Pomarancio and Peruzzi in the second chapel, and by Vasari in the fourth. In 1503 Bramante was commissioned to build the famous "Tempietto" to commemorate the martyrdom of St. Peter. It has a circular plan that consists of a sanctuary surrounded by an ambulatory with 16 granite columns. An upper entablature and a small dome, whose drum is enlivened by alternating rectangular and curved niches, bestow St. Peter with an air of harmony and monumentality in spite of its small size. In its classical form and perfect proportions it symbolizes the synthesis of ancient and Christian Rome.

⓯ SAN CRISOGONO

Piazza Sonnino, 44
☎ 06 58 10 00 76
🚌 H, 23, 280, 780
🚊 8
Ⓜ Circo Massimo
Opening hours: 7 a.m.–12 p.m., 4:15–7:30 p.m., Mon–Sat; 8:30 a.m.–1 p.m.,

4:15–7:30 p.m. Sun

This is an ancient "parish" church (*titulus*), whose early Christian phase is visible in the lower part, while the upper part is a 17th-century transformation of the 12th-century building. The original 5th-century church is parallel with it, but further to the left in relation to the medieval one. It features three naves, ending in a wide apse. The *Confessio* in the area of the sanctuary dates from the 8th century.

⓰ SANTA MARIA IN TRASTEVERE

Via della Paglia, 14/c
☎ 06 58 14 802
🚌 H, 23, 280, 780
🚊 8
Ⓜ Circo Massimo
Opening hours: 7:30 a.m.–8 p.m.

This ancient "parish" church, built by Pope Julius I (337–352), has maintained the medieval appearance imposed on it by Pope Innocent II (1138–1148). The portico and the façade were rebuilt in the 18th century. Outside it is a 13th-century mosaic of the Virgin enthroned. In the center of the wooden ceiling is Domenichino's *Assumption of the Blessed Virgin*, dated to 1617. In the center of the apse, which dates from about the late 12th century, is *Christ crowning the Virgin Mary among saints and Popes*. There are mosaic panels between the windows, made by Pietro Cavallini in 1291 and representing stories of the Virgin. Finally, the 6th- or 7th-century painting on the altar, in encaustic on wood, a technique typical of Roman painting, called the *Madonna della Clemenza*, is especially of interest.

⓱ Santa Cecilia

Piazza di Santa Cecilia, 22
☎ 06 58 99 289
🚌 H, 23, 44, 280
🚊 8
Ⓜ Circo Massimo
Opening hours: 9:40 a.m.–12:30 p.m., 4–6:30 p.m.
The fresco by Cavallini can be visited 10 a.m.–12:35 p.m. Mon–Sat

Recent digging has identified significant elements, including the 5th-century baptistery, which had reused a building with an apse from the time of Trajan, situated under the Chapel of the Relics. The remains also included parts of a house from the Imperial era, located under the present church. A late account of St. Cecilia's martyrdom says that was where she lived, and that the house was acquired by the Church, at her wish. Pope Paschal I (817–824) rebuilt the church and had the martyr's remains brought there from the catacombs of San Callisto. The church today looks as it did in the 18th century, although works were carried out at various times, particularly at the turn of the 13th century (in the portico, the bell-tower, the right wing of the convent and the cloisters) and in the 16th century. The church is flanked by the convent of the sisters and there is a broad medieval courtyard in front of it. It features three naves, divided by pillars, which (since the 19th century) encompass the 24 original Corinthian columns. The vault has paintings by Sebastiano Conca from about 1727, representing the *Coronation of St. Cecilia*. A corridor leading off the right-hand nave leads to the "Chapel of the Bath," possibly the bath where the saint was martyred. It contains a tondo by Guido Reni of the *Marriage of St. Cecilia and Valerian*, and above the altar a canvas by Reni of the *Beheading of the saint* (dated to 1603). In front of Arnolfo di Cambio's canopy of 1293 stands a statue of St. Cecilia (1600), by Stefano Maderno. The mosaic in the apse (circa 820), is of high quality. It shows Christ blessing, crowned by the hand of God, and at his sides St. Paul, St. Cecilia and the Pope who paid for the church, carrying a model of it, and Sts. Peter, Valerian and Agatha. Below, twelve lambs surrounding the Lamb of God are shown leaving the cities of Jerusalem and Bethlehem. The nuns' choir contains a late 13th-century fresco of the *Last Judgement* by Pietro Cavallini. Also preserved here are paintings of the *Annunciation*, *St. Christopher*, *Jacob's Dream* and the *Deception of Isaac*.

⓲ SANTA MARIA DEL POPOLO

Piazza del Popolo, 12
☎ 06 36 10 836
🚌 95, 117, 119, 490, 495
🚋 2
Ⓜ Flaminio
Opening hours: 7:30
a.m.–12 p.m., 4–7 p.m.
Mon–Sat; 7:30 a.m.–

1:30 p.m., 4:30–7:30 p.m.
Sun

In 1099 Pope Paschal II
built a chapel in honor
of the Virgin Mary above
the Roman tombs of
the Domitii family. The
church was enlarged by
Gregory IX, and rebuilt,
perhaps by Andrea
Bregno, between 1472
and 1478 as ordered by
Sixtus IV, thus creating a
museum with works by
the greatest artists of the
Renaissance and the 17th
century. Bernini carried
out extensive alterations to
the façade and the interior.
Particularly of interest
are the chapels of the
nobility: the Chigi Chapel
(designed by Raphael with
an altarpiece by Sebastiano
del Piombo), the Della
Rovere Chapel (with
frescoes by Pinturicchio
from 1485–1489), and
above all the Cerasi

Chapel, with two canvases
by Caravaggio, the
Conversion of St. Paul and
the *Crucifixion of St. Peter*
(1601–1602). Situated
behind the altar are the
funerary monuments of
Ascanio Sforza (1505)
and Girolamo Basso Della
Rovere (1507), by Andrea
Sansovino. Above it are
the two earliest stained
glass windows in Rome,
with stories of the *Virgin
and the Childhood of
Christ*, executed by the
Frenchman Guillaume
de Marcillat (1509). The
Cesi Chapel preserves
the altarpiece of the
Assumption by Annibale
Carracci (1601). On the
high altar, dated to 1627,
is a t13h-century painting,
the Madonna del Popolo,
traditionally said to have
been painted by St. Luke.
In the apse are frescoes by
Pinturicchio, representing
the *Coronation of the
Virgin, Evangelists, sibyls
and Doctors of the Church*.
Bramante contributed to
the transformation of the
choir between 1500 and
1509.

⓳ TWIN CHURCHES OF PIAZZA DEL POPOLO

Santa Maria dei Miracoli:
Via del Corso, 528
☎ 06 36 10 250
Opening hours: 7 a.m.–1
p.m., 4–7:30 p.m. Mon–
Sat; 8 a.m.–1 p.m., 4:30–
7:30 p.m. Sun and holidays
Santa Maria in Montesanto:
Via del Babuino, 197
☎ 06 36 10 594
Opening hours: 4–7 Mon–
Sat; 11 a.m.–12:30 p.m.
Sun
🚌 95, 117, 119, 490,
495, 628, 926
Ⓜ Flaminio

In the Middle Ages, in
what is now Piazza del
Popolo, a gate, called Porta
San Valentino, opened
up in the Aurelian Walls,
and from it ran the long,
straight Via Lata (Via del
Corso). At the start of the
16th century, Pope Leo
X (Medici) (1513–1521)
commissioned Raphael
and Sangallo to create a
road from the road from
Porto di Ripetta to Piazza
del Popolo (Via Leonina).
A few years later, in 1523,
what is currently Via del
Babuino (Via Paolina) was
started by Clement VII
and completed by Paul
III. It ran alonside the
slopes of the Pincian hill
as far as Piazza di Spagna;
hence, it was one of the
most important pieces of
urban planning in Rome
(the so-called "Trident").
Before it was "furnished"
by Valadier, Sixtus V
commissioned Domenico
Fontana to place there a
large obelisk that originally

had lain in the Circus Maximus (it is the oldest in Rome after the one at the Lateran, 36.50 meters high including its base). But it was Alexander VII Chigi (1655-1667) who had the spectacular idea of building the twin churches at the head of the "Trident." The scenario was worthy of Rome's monumentality, and it also attested to the city's sacredness. The churches were begun by Carlo Rainaldi and completed by Bernini and Carlo Fontana, and although they appear to be identical, they are actually rather different. They each have a portico with a classical tympanum, evoking the solemnity of the Pantheon, and are covered by a large dome with "fish-scale" tiles. Each has a short bell-tower, offering a wonderful example of Baroque design, and creating a type of building on a central plan particularly well suited to an urban site that cannot

be extended lengthways. The architectural elements produce an effect of grandeur designed to create a powerful impression of monumentality. On the right, towards Via Ripetta, is Santa Maria dei Miracoli, completed in 1597, which commemorates the miraculous image of the Virgin preserved at its high altar. It is circular, with two chapels on each side and an octagonal dome, and has sculptures by Antonio Raggi. On the left, towards Via del Babuino, is Santa Maria in Montesanto, built on the site of an older church belonging to the Sicilian Carmelite order of Monte Santo. It was completed in 1675, on an elliptical plan, and includes three chapels on each side and a twelve-sided dome. It is celebrated for the "Mass of the Artists," commemorating the Stations of the Cross, for which the models were made by great modern Italian sculptors.

20 SANTI AMBROGIO E CARLO AL CORSO

Via del Corso, 437
📞 06 68 28 101
🚌 81, 117, 492, 628, 926
Ⓜ Spagna
Opening hours: 7 a.m.–7 p.m.

Rising up on the site of San Niccolò del Tufo, this church was rebuilt under the name of Sant'Ambrogio dei Lombardi, and in 1612 Onorio Longhi was given the task of enlarging it. On that occasion it was dedicated to St. Ambrose and St. Charles Borromeo. When Longhi died he had only designed the project, a façade with two bell-towers, a large dome and four smaller ones. His son, Martino Longhi the Younger, took over, and in 1651 Pietro da Cortona made the apse, the dome and the high altar. The façade, crowned by a tympanum, was completed in 1684 by G. Battista Menicucci and Mario da Canepina. The interior, a Latin cross with friezes and stucco decoration, is divided into three naves by pillars with pilaster strips in fake marble. The two side naves go round the sacristy, creating an ambulatory, the only one in Rome, recalling the one in Milan cathedral. Its most interesting feature is a fresco in the central vault depicting the *Fall of the Rebel Angels*, executed by Giacinto Brandi. The altarpiece, the *Glory of Sts. Ambrose and Charles*, was painted by Maratta in 1690. Behind the altar is a reliquary with the heart of St. Charles Borromeo. The left transept leads to the 16th-century oratory of Sant'Ambrogio, built above the church of San Niccolò del Tufo.

㉑ SAN LORENZO IN LUCINA

Via in Lucina, 16/a
📞 06 68 71 494
🚌 81, 117, 119, 492, 628
Ⓜ Spagna
Opening hours: 8:30 a.m.–8 p.m.

The epithet "in Lucina" derives from the name of the Roman matron who gave shelter to Pope St. Marcellus (308–309) when he was being persecuted by the Emperor Maxentius. Her house was located in an area that was important in Imperial Rome, near the temple of Hadrian (Piazza di Pietra), the temple of the Sun (now lost) and the *Ara Pacis Augustae* (later transferred to the Lungotevere). The successive church was built on the ruins of the house, around the 4th century. Pope St. Damasus was elected in it in 366, and it was restored in 685 by Benedict II, in 780 by Adrian I and 1112 by Paschal II, who completely rebuilt it, adorning it with the Romanesque bell-tower whose top three stories have double mullioned windows. In 1650 Cosimo Fanzago extensively restored the interior leaving intact the

façade that had been built under Paschal II, with the columns of its portico bearing medieval plaques and marble fragments, and its doorway flanked by lions supporting pillars. There is a single nave with side chapels, and in the apse, the marble throne of Paschal II. The coffered ceiling dates from 1857 (Pope Pius IX). On the high altar, which has six Corinthian columns of black marble and a curved tympanum above, is Guido Reni's painting of *Christ on the Cross*. Preserved in an urn below the altar is the gridiron on which St. Lawrence was martyred. The 4th chapel on the right was designed in the 17th century by Gian Lorenzo Bernini, who also made the bust of the doctor Gabriele Fonseca. To the left of the entrance is the baptistery executed by Sardi, truly a jewel of 17th-century architecture.

㉒ SANTO SPIRITO IN SASSIA

Via dei Penitenzieri, 12
📞 06 68 79 310
🚌 23, 34, 46, 62, 64, 98, 870, 881
Ⓜ Ottaviano, San Pietro
Opening hours: 7:30 a.m.–12 p.m. (9:30 a.m.–1 p.m. Sun), 3–7:30 p.m.

The church of Santo Spirito in Sassia, annexed to the hospital of the same name, rises up on the very same spot where in Carolingian times King Ine of Wessex built the Schola dei Saxonum, a charitable foundation near St. Peter's for pilgrims

of Saxon nationality. Originally under the authority of the church of Santa Maria in Sassia, it was rebuilt in the 12th century and again in 1475, when it was annexed to the hospital dedicated to the Holy Spirit and built by Sixtus IV to support poor pilgrims in that year's Jubilee. Devastated in the sack of Rome in 1527, it was rebuilt between 1538 and 1545 by Antonio da Sangallo the Younger, under Pope Paul III. The exterior dates from the time of Sixtus V (1585–1590), but the bell-tower from that of Sixtus IV (1471–1484). It has a single nave, with ten apsidal chapels round the sides, and it also features pieces of frescoes by various 16th- and 17th-century painters. The choir, with an organ dated to 1547, is of high quality. In the adjacent hospital, which retains its early construction, the rotating hatch where foundling babies were left can still be seen.

㉓ CHIESA NUOVA

Via del Governo Vecchio, 134
🚌 46, 62, 64
Ⓜ Spagna
Opening hours: 8 a.m.–12 p.m. (1 p.m. Sun), 4:30–7 p.m.

The original building, probably founded by Gregory the Great in the 6th century, rose up on a depression in the ground, where bogs and ponds formed. In antiquity it was called *Tarentum*, and it was believed that a wide-mouthed cave was the entrance to hell. In 1575 St. Philip Neri, who lived in the adjoining rooms and was in charge of the church, had a new church built—hence the name—to a design by Matteo Bartolini and Martino Longhi the Elder, who embellished the interior with gold, stucco, friezes and paintings. The broad, high façade, completed by Fausto Rughesi in 1605, has two stories of pilaster strips, crowned by a triangular tympanum, a doorway

with double columns and a high entablature and, in the center of the upper storey, a window with a balustrade. The Latin-cross interior has three naves, with five communicating chapels on each side. The church preserves some very fine works of art, including the fresco on the ceiling of the main nave by Pietro da Cortona (1664–1665). Depicted is the miracle of the Virgin, who warned St. Philip in a dream of the imminent collapse of the church roof; it was thus repaired immediately and saved the lives of many of the faithful. Also of interest are the two huge paintings by Rubens (1606–1608) to the sides of the apse (the Madonna and Child covers a miraculous image of the Virgin), the 17th-century oval paintings above the round windows of the side chapels, depicting events from the Old and New Testaments, and the Cappella Spada, by Carlo Rainaldi, in the left transept, with the *Madonna Enthroned with Sts. Charles Borromeo and Ignatius* (1685), executed by Maratta. The small chapel of San Filippo Neri (whose body lies in the urn below the altar) to the left of the apse, is a Baroque jewel, with mother-of-pearl, marble, gold, bronze and stucco decorations. To the left of the church is the oratory of the Philippines, started by Borromini in 1637 on the site of the original one where St. Philip organized the first sacred performances (religious music for soloists and choir). It is a perfect example of the aesthetic use of space, and has a concave façade, accentuated by the central balcony which stands against a large, barely curved niche. The decoration of the interior directly conceals the courtyards, the great stair, the atrium and the various rooms, including the oval room and the Vallicellian Library, the oldest public library in Rome. The whole complex remains connected with the figure of St. Philip Neri, and his concept of a profound popular piety, based on the realistic relationship of life and living faith. The enormous impact of this idea, especially in the ancient city of Rome where he fervently spread the Gospel, and the warmth with which leading Roman families supported his work, created this "ideal city" (consisting of the church, the convent, the library and the oratory), in one of Rome's oldest and most densely populated quarters.

㉔ SANT'AGNESE IN AGONE

Via di Santa Maria dell'Anima, 30
☎ 06 68 19 21 34
🚌 46, 62, 64, 70, 81, 87, 116, 492, 628
Ⓜ Spagna
Opening hours: 9:30 a.m.–12:30 p.m., 4–7 p.m. Tue to Sun

In the middle of the western side of Piazza Navona, on the very spot where the Saint was martyred, exposed naked to scorn but covered by her own hair that had miraculously grown, an oratory was dedicated to her: the added *in agone* derives from the ancient stadium of Domitian (*Campus Agonis*), of 86 AD. Pope Calixtus II turned it into a church with three naves, until in 1652, Innocent X Pamphilj, whose palace adjoined the church, decided to make it look grand, with the help of the architects Girolamo and Carlo Rainaldi. But the Pope was not satisfied with the design, and gave the work to Borromini, whose façade had more

㉕ Sant'Andrea della Valle

Piazza Vidoni, 6
☏ 06 68 61 339
🚌 H, 40, 46, 62, 64, 70, 81, 87, 116, 186, 492, 628
🚋 8
Ⓜ Spagna
Opening hours: 7:30 a.m.– 12 p.m., 4:30–7:30 p.m.

Rising up on this site was the ancient church of San Sebastiano (where the Roman matron Luciana is traditionally held to have found the pierced body of the saint and martyr), with next to it the palace of the noble Sienese family of the Piccolomini; Costanza, Duchess of Amalfi, left it to the Theatine Fathers in 1582 so that they could build a church dedicated to St. Andrew, patron saint of Amalfi. But a few years later Sixtus V started his major widening of the papal road; palace and church were destroyed and the Theatines retired to San Silvestro on the Quirinal hill. The present church is an example of the transition from Counter-

movement, with an oval stair leading up from the piazza and elaborate bell-towers. But when Innocent X died in 1655, work proceeded so slowly under his nephew Camillo that Borromini resigned in favour of Carlo Rainaldi. When Camillo died, his wife took over the project, calling in Gian Lorenzo Bernini, who altered Borromini's original design, of which only the concave façade, with its single order of pilasters and columns, and the lofty dome which seems to lean dangerously, remain. Bernini was responsible for the high pediment, topped by an attic story. The interior preserves Rainaldi's Greek-cross plan, an octagon set in a square, with large niches at the crossing of the deeper horizontal with the vertical arms, on the dome rests, supported on Borromini's eight large columns of red marble. It has frescoes painted by Ciro Ferri, Sebastiano Corbellini and Baciccia in the late 17th century. There are reliefs and statues on the seven altars, and to the left of the high altar is the crypt containing the body of Innocent X. His 18th-century funerary monument, by Maini, is above the main entrance. In the basement of the church are Roman ruins which were popularly believed to lead to the catacombs of Sant'Agnese on the Via Nomentana.

Reformation to Baroque. It was designed in 1590 by Pier Paolo Olivieri, but the interior and the dome (at 16.10 meters in diameter and 80 meters high the largest in Rome after St. Peter's) were built to a plan by Carlo Maderno. The façade is by Carlo Rainaldi. It has five lower and three upper bays, divided by pairs of projecting columns, a central window, with a tympanum, above, and a doorway with the arms of Pope Alexander VII Chigi. He commissioned Ercole Ferrara to make two statues of angels to be placed on the volutes connecting the lower and upper orders, but only one was completed. The lantern of the dome is attributed to Borromini; it was his first work. The interior is a Latin cross, with an apse, a nave with a barrel vault and four side chapels, and a transept supporting Maderno's dome. It contains 17th-century works of art such as Giovanni Lanfranco's 1625 fresco in the crown, the *Glories of Paradise*; in the pendentives, the *Evangelists*, painted in 1628 by Domenichino, who also painted the *Stories of St. Andrew* in the apse; and the apse by Mattia Preti, with the *Crucifixion and Burial of St. Andrew*. In 1614 the tombs of the Piccolomini Popes (Pius II, 1464, and Pius III, 1503), were brought here from St.

Peter's and placed at the far end of the nave. The significant side chapels are the Lancellotti by Carlo Fontana, the Strani by Giacomo Della Porta, and the Barberini, with sculptures by Pietro Bernini.

26 SANT'IVO ALLA SAPIENZA

Corso Rinascimento, 40
☎ 06 36 12 562
🚌 40, 46, 64, 70, 81, 87, 115, 116, 186, 492, 628
Ⓜ Spagna
Opening hours: 9 a.m.–12 p.m. Sun

The edifice of the University of Rome La Sapienza, founded in 1303 by Boniface VIII and enlarged by Alexander VI (1492–1503), was rebuilt during the papacies of Gregory XIII (1572–1585) and Sixtus V (1585–1590). The work was carried out by Giacomo Della Porta and completed by Francesco Borromini, who built the university chapel, consecrated in 1660. Borromini had to adapt his design to the

work already in place, including part of the façade, which now forms the background of the 16th-century courtyard: the two stories of arches continue along the wall of the church, and are made lighter by a series of niches with windows. The tall multi-lobed drum, divided by numerous pilaster strips, is topped by a stepped dome with ribs of inverted arches and ends in a spiral lantern. Inspired by the Tower of Babel, it is crowned with wrought-iron work (the cage, the orb, the dove and the cross). The interior is perhaps the epitome of Roman Baroque, and is built on an unusual plan (two superimposed equilateral triangles, with concave and convex parts closing the sides). It is said to have been inspired by the heraldic bee from the coat of arms of Pope Urban VIII Barberini. Three large niches alternate with three smaller ones against which are set the Corinthian columns supporting the heavy cornice. They are continued into the ribs, which become narrower and join at the base of the lantern, dividing the dome into six segments. The interior, as designed by Borromini, is white, with stucco decoration, and has an altarpiece by Pietro da Cortona, depicting St. Ivo.

㉗ SAN LUIGI DEI FRANCESI

Piazza San Luigi dei Francesi, 5
☎ 06 68 82 71
🚌 70, 81, 87, 116, 186, 492, 628
Ⓜ Barberini
Opening hours: 10 a.m.–12:30 p.m., 4–7 p.m.,

closed Thursday afternoon

The monks of the abbey of Farfa came into possession of this site, full of monuments from the early Empire (the Baths of Agrippa and of Nero), and kept it until the early sixteenth century. It was then taken over by the Medici, who had built the Palazzo Madama there. In 1518, Cardinal Giulio de' Medici (Clement VII) commissioned Jean de Chenevières to build the new church that the French community wanted, but after the sack of Rome in 1527 it was completed by Domenico Fontana (1589). The façade, by Giacomo Della Porta, is in two stories, with a triangular tympanum, three doors and two statues in niches (below is the salamander of Francis I). The interior was decorated by Dérizet, with five chapels on each side. The 5th on the left was painted by Caravaggio between 1597 and 1602 with three scenes from the life of St. Matthew: *The Calling*, *The Martyrdom* and *Matthew and the Angel*. This is the French national church.

㉘ PANTHEON (SANTA MARIA AD MARTYRES)

Piazza della Rotonda
☎ 06 68 30 02 30
🚌 81, 115, 116, 492, 628
Ⓜ Barberini

Of all the ancient Roman buildings this is the best preserved. This is because in the time of Pope Boniface IV it was turned into the church of Santa Maria ad Martyres. Its original plan was rectangular, and the façade faced in the opposite direction from the present one. It was built by Marcus Vipsanius Agrippa, Consul in 27 BC, in honor of his father-in-law Augustus, and dedicated to the dynastic gods of the Julio-Claudian family (Mars, Venus and Julius Caesar). It was rebuilt in its present form in the time of Hadrian. The Emperor had an inscription in bronze letters placed on the architrave, recording the first builder, Marcus Agrippa. A vestibule with eight granite columns, topped by a tympanum originally ornamented with a crowned eagle, leads through a bronze door (the original door, but heavily restored), into the circular interior (which gives the Pantheon its popular name, the *Rotonda*). It is covered by a coffered concrete dome that becomes lighter towards the top, where pumice was used. With a diameter of 43.30

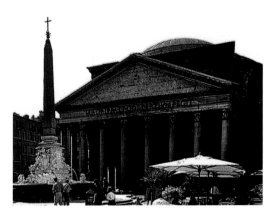

meters, it is the largest masonry dome ever built. To lighten the weight, the walls are interrupted by blind arches, which can be seen clearly from outside. The interior walls are broken by rectangular and semi-circular niches framed by polychrome marble columns. The upper part of the walls, and the floor, are also in marble, making a powerful visual impact.

㉙ SANTA MARIA SOPRA MINERVA

Via della Minerva, 42
📞 06 67 93 926
🚌 81, 115, 116, 492, 628
Ⓜ Barberini
Opening hours: 7 a.m.–7 p.m. Mon–Sat; 8 a.m.–1 p.m., 4–7 p.m. Sun
Cloister currently closed for restoration work

The church of Santa Maria sopra Minerva, locatec close to the Pantheon,

dominates the Piazza della Minerva. It was built in the late 3rd or first half of the 4th century on the ruins of a temple,

probably dedicated to Minerva Chalcidica. The many works of art preserved there include the fresco decoration of the Carafa Chapel, in the right-hand part of the transept, with Filippino Lippi's *Annunciation* and *Assumption*, painted between 1488 and 1493. On view in the sanctuary is Michelangelo's statue of the *Risen Christ* (1519–1520), and in the left-hand part is the slab from the tomb of Fra Angelico, executed by Isaia da Pisa.

㉚ SANT'IGNAZIO

Via del Caravita, 8/a
📞 06 67 94 406
🚌 117, 492, 628
Ⓜ Barberini
Opening hours: 7:30 a.m.–7 p.m.

The church, built between 1626 and 1650, overlooks the piazza enclosed by the two small palaces designed by Filippo Raguzzini (1728), forming one of the most characteristic ensembles of 18th-century urban planning. It was designed by the Jesuit Father Orazio Grassi, at a time when the Jesuits were at the height of their prestige, because of the recent canonization of Ignatius. The church is the logical completion to the church of Gesù, with parallels to it in the façade (late 17th-century by Alessandro Algardi), with its two stories of Corinthian columns and pilaster strips, and

cornices, frontispiece, side volutes, large window and tympanum, all in bold chiaroscuro. There are also similarities in the interior, with its wide nave and apse dominating a Latin-cross plan whose impact is modified by the Baroque decoration and the sumptuousness of the altars in the transept. The fresco painting of the great vault of the nave is the largest and most accomplished work of Andrea Pozzo (1685). It shows the *Glory of St. Ignatius* entering Paradise where he is welcomed by Christ and the Virgin while a ray of light strikes him, splitting so that it reaches the four corners of the world; the effect of perspective creates an illusion of open colonnades through which the sky can be seen. Just as spectacular is the impact of the false dome painted by Pozzo on a canvas 17 meters in diameter.

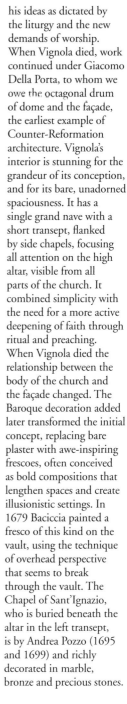

③ CHURCH OF GESÙ

Piazza del Gesù
📞 06 69 70 01
🚌 H, 46, 62, 64, 70, 81, 87, 186, 492, 628, 810
🚋 8
Ⓜ Barberini
Opening hours: 7 a.m.–12:30 p.m. (7:30 a.m.–1 p.m. Sun), 4–7:45 p.m.

St. Ignatius Loyola, who born in the late 15th century, founded the Society of Jesus in 1537, which Paul III transformed into the Jesuit Order. Since their first church (Santa Maria della Strada, behind Palazzo Venezia)

was very small, Ignatius wanted to build another to be dedicated to the Holy Name of Jesus, destined to become the prototype for churches between the Counter-Reformation and the Baroque, imitated in Italy and abroad. Work was suspended in 1551 and again in 1554, but, on the death of St. Ignatius (1556), his fellow-Jesuit Francis Borgia handed the project over to Vignola. Work began in 1568, taking account of St. Charles Borromeo's *Instructions on religious building works*. He believed the artist should serve the priest, and interpret his ideas as dictated by the liturgy and the new demands of worship. When Vignola died, work continued under Giacomo Della Porta, to whom we owe the octagonal drum of dome and the façade, the earliest example of Counter-Reformation architecture. Vignola's interior is stunning for the grandeur of its conception, and for its bare, unadorned spaciousness. It has a single grand nave with a short transept, flanked by side chapels, focusing all attention on the high altar, visible from all parts of the church. It combined simplicity with the need for a more active deepening of faith through ritual and preaching. When Vignola died the relationship between the body of the church and the façade changed. The Baroque decoration added later transformed the initial concept, replacing bare plaster with awe-inspiring frescoes, often conceived as bold compositions that lengthen spaces and create illusionistic settings. In 1679 Baciccia painted a fresco of this kind on the vault, using the technique of overhead perspective that seems to break through the vault. The Chapel of Sant'Ignazio, who is buried beneath the altar in the left transept, is by Andrea Pozzo (1695 and 1699) and richly decorated in marble, bronze and precious stones.

❸❷ SAN MARCELLO AL CORSO

Piazza di San Marcello, 5
📞 06 69 93 01
🚌 62, 63, 81, 85, 95, 117, 119, 160, 175, 492, 628
Ⓜ Barberini
Opening hours: 7 a.m.–12 p.m. (from 10 a.m. Sat,

from 9 a.m. Sun), 4–7 p.m.

Legend has it that Pope St. Marcellus (308–309), sentenced by Maxentius to look after the horses at the station of the Imperial mail on the Via Lata (now Via del Corso), was freed by the people and hidden in the nearby house of the matron Lucina, which became a place of pilgrimage. He was arrested again by the Emperor and imprisoned in the same stables, and died in 309. Boniface I was consecrated Pope in the early church in 418. It was restored by Adrian I in the 8th century, and the battered body of Cola di Rienzo was hung up in the apse in 1354. Only the outer walls and the 15th-century wooden

crucifix from the high altar, now kept in the chapel of the same name, survived the fire of 1519. Money collected to restore the church was used in 1527 to convince Charles V not to plunder it. It was given its present form (1592) by Antonio Sangallo the Younger, to a design by Jacopo Sansovino that removed the side naves and transept. The concave façade (1682) is by Carlo Fontana; the doorway is flanked by three columns on each side, supporting a curvilinear tympanum. The upper level is tied to the lower by two palm leaves. The curve of this façade increases the visual impact of its architectural elements, in harmony with the sculpture (the work of Antonio Raggi dated to 1686). The interior has a single nave, with five chapels on each side, and frescoes by G. B. Ricci of Novara. Under the altar is a 3rd-century marble memorial stone, decorated on the front with 12th-century *opus sectile* mosaic and used to contain martyrs' relics.

❸❸ SANTI APOSTOLI

Piazza Santi Apostoli
📞 06 69 95 71
🚌 H, 40, 64, 70, 170
Ⓜ Barberini
Opening hours: 7 a.m.–12 p.m., 4–7.15 p.m.

Although an early building is said to date back to Pope Julius I (337–352), the church was founded by

Pelagius I (556–561) after the Goths were driven out, and John III (561–574) completed it and dedicated it to the Apostles James and Philip. Inside the ancient church was an image of the Saviour painted by Melozzo da Forlì, which Clement XI brought to the Quirinal Palace. In the sanctuary was a tabernacle of the Eucharist, and on the high altar, the *tegurium* (a canopy supported on four porphyry columns). It was restored by Stephen V (885–891), but Pope Martin V Colonna was responsible for reconstructing it in 1417, after it had fallen into ruin and been abandoned following an earthquake in 1348. The whole of the surrounding area belonged to the Colonna family, including the palace, in which the Pope stayed for a time (while the Lateran Palace was being repaired). It had been built to mark the restoration of the church, considered almost a family chapel. At the end of the 1400s, the architect Baccio Pontelli, at the service of Pope Sixtus IV, transformed the façade, creating the loggia with nine arches on two levels, of which the upper was later walled up by Carlo Rainaldi in the second half of the 17th century. Rainaldi conceived the Baroque windows and the balustrade with statues of Christ and the twelve Apostles. It was restored again by Carlo and Francesco Fontana under Clement XI (1700–1721), and in 1827 Valadier designed its present plain, very tall Neoclassical façade with its huge central window and tympanum. From the 16th century the name of the basilica was extended to include all the Apostles.

Under the portico is one of the most beautiful Imperial Roman eagles, from the first century AD, a lion supporting a pillar, signed by Vassalletto (13th century), and early Christian fragments and tombstones. The interior is divided into three naves by large pillars with matching Corinthian pilaster strips; it has three domed chapels on each side, and is filled with works of art. On the vault of the central nave is a fresco by Baciccia, showing the *Triumph of the Order of St. Francis* (1707), and above the sanctuary, one by G. Odazzi, representing the *Expulsion of the Rebel Angels* (1709). On the far wall is a canvas by D. Muratori, of the *Martyrdom of Sts.*

Philip and James. To the right of the apse is the Chapel of the Crucifixion divided into three small naves by eight spiral columns from the original church. Two 16th-century cloisters complete the church complex. To the left of the basilica is the Santi Apostoli Palace (15th century), belonging to the Holy See, with corner towers and marble windows, possibly built by Giuliano da Sangallo (1478) for the future Pope Julius II.

㉞ Santa Maria di Loreto

Piazza di Santa Maria di Loreto, 26
☎ 06 67 92 235
🚌 44, 46, 60, 84, 85, 87, 175, 715, 716
Ⓜ Colosseo, Cavour

The church was started

by Antonio da Sangallo the Younger in 1507 and finished by Jacopo del Duca, following the demolition of another church given to the Bakers' Guild by Pope Alexander VI. Its f15th-century altarpiece by Antoniazzo Romano, depicting the *Madonna with St. Sebastian and St. Roch*, came from that church, and now stands on Onorio Longhi's altar. The exterior is a cube, and its dome is topped by an unusual lantern (the crickets cage). The interior is octagonal, with chapels in the niches on the oblique sides, and a deep sanctuary.

㉟ Santissimo Nome di Maria

Foro Traiano, 89
☎ 06 67 98 013
🚌 44, 46, 60, 84, 85, 87, 175, 715, 716
Ⓜ Colosseo, Cavour

On the site of a little 15th-century church belonging to the Company of San Bernardo an even smaller one was built (1683). The present church, on a central plan, was built next to it in 1736. It has a square foundation with rounded corners, a high drum and a dome in eight sections. The elliptical interior includes seven small chapels, decorated in polychrome marble, and an image of the Virgin, at one time housed in the oratory of San Lorenzo in Laterano and taken in solemn procession from the now destroyed church of San Bernardo to its present place.

③⑥ SAN MARCO

Piazza San Marco, 48
☎ 06 67 95 205
🚌 40, 62, 63, 64, 81, 95, 160, 170, 628, 715
Ⓜ Colosseo
Opening hours: 8:30 a.m.–12 p.m., Tue–Sat; 4–6:30 p.m. Mon–Sat; 9 a.m.–1 p.m., 4–8 p.m. Sun

This is one of Rome's oldest churches, probably founded by Pope Marcus (336), on the very spot where the Evangelist is said to have lived while he was in Rome. It was built on the basilical plan, with an orientation similar to today's. In the 5th century it was destroyed and rebuilt, facing in the opposite direction. In the 6th and 7th centuries it was repeatedly sacked by Goths, Lombards and Byzantines. It was rebuilt by Adrian I (772–795), with its present orientation, but immediately flooded when the Tiber broke its banks in 791. Gregory IV (827–844) restored it, adding the mosaics in the apse, and in 1100 it acquired its bell-tower and a now lost canopy. Cardinal Pietro Barbo, who became Pope Paul II (1464–1471), transformed it, turning it into the church of the Venetians in Rome and the most interesting building from the beginning of the Roman Renaissance. The façade is by Leon Battista Alberti, who was at that time at the service of the papal court. It has a portico of three arches, marked by vigorous piers with half-columns back to back. The very elegant Loggia of Benedictions above it, with broader arches and slender pilaster strips, was completed by Giuliano da Maiano in 1471. Paul II then had his residence built next to the church. It was called Palazzo Venezia because it was the residence of the Venetian ambassadors. Under the portico in front of the church are the Renaissance door of Isaia da Pisa, the remains of the ancient canopy and a curious inscription on a medieval well-head, cursing anyone who sold the water drawn from it. The 15th-century interior features three naves, and a wooden ceiling from the 2nd half of the century, possibly the oldest in Rome, with that of Santa Maria Maggiore. The 9th-century mosaic in the apse shows *Christ blessing, five saints and the donor, Pope Gregory V*. Under the mullioned windows of Paul II, in the central nave, are 18th-century frescoes and the funerary monument of the child Leonardo Pesaro, by Antonio Canova (1796). On the altar of Pietro da Cortona's Chapel of the Sacrament is the portrait of *Pope St. Marcus* by Melozzo da Forlì. His portrait of *St. Mark the Evangelist* is in the sacristy, where there are also traces of a fresco from the school of Cavallini.

㊲ ORATORY OF THE SANTISSIMO SACRAMENTO

Piazza Poli, 11
☎ 06 67 97 541
🚌 56, 58, 60, 62, 81, 85
Ⓜ Barberini

Built by order of the brotherhood of the same name during the papacy of Gregory XIII (1572–1585), the church was completed in 1681 with the addition of the façade, by Carlo Rainaldi. Under Benedict XIII (1724–1730) it was completely reconstructed by Gregorini and adorned with its current interior decoration. The outside of the doorway has two pairs of half-columns supporting a broken curvilinear pediment, surmounted by statues representing Faith and Hope. The interior, which is elliptical, with a dome, has on its walls pairs of fluted pilaster strips under a large projecting cornice. The 18th-century *Holy Family* on the altar is by Trevisani.

㊳ SANTA MARIA IMMACOLATA A VIA VENETO

Via Veneto, 27
☎ 06 48 71 11 85
🚌 52, 53, 61, 62, 63, 80, 95, 116, 119, 175
Ⓜ Barberini
Opening hours: 7 a.m.–12 p.m., 3–7 p.m.

The church on Via Veneto, also known as as Santa Maria della Concezione and Chiesa dei Cappuccini, has a single nave with ten side-chapels. It was built to a design by Antonio Casoni from 1626 to 1631, but the façade and the steps in front were modified in the 20th century. The first chapel on the right contains two paintings, Guido Reni's *Archangel Michael* (1630, see illustration) and *Christ Mocked*, by Gherardo Delle Notti. Also of interest are *St. Francis with the Stigmata*, by Domenichino and the tomb (1646) of Cardinal Antonio Barberini, who

funded the church, with its famous inscription "Here lie dust and ashes, nothing else." In the convent are Caravaggio's *St. Francis* (1603), and the *Nazarene* by Jacopo Palma the Younger. The adjacent cemetery of the Capuchins has five chapels made up of the bones and skulls of 4,000 friars who died between 1528 and 1870.

㊴ SANT'ANDREA AL QUIRINALE

Via del Quirinale, 29
☎ 06 47 44 872
🚌 71, 116, 117
Ⓜ Barberini
Opening hours: 8:30 a.m.– 12 p.m., 3:30–7 p.m.

In 1658, Cardinal Pamphilj, nephew of Pope Innocent X, paid for a

church to be built for the adjoining Jesuit convent. Bernini was put in charge, and work was completed thirteen years later. The façade consists of a single story, with a semicircular vestibule supported on two columns and flanked by two tall pilaster strips which support the tympanum. The interior is elliptical in shape, decorated with gilded stucco and marble. Four chapels and four deep niches open off the central area; they contain 17th- and 18th-century paintings. The dome is coffered and gilded, and decorated with friezes and stucco. Under the altar is a bronze and lapis lazuli urn, containing the Saint's body.

④ SAN CARLO ALLE QUATTRO FONTANE

Via del Quirinale, 23
📞 06 48 83 261
🚌 60, 61, 62, 116, 117, 175, 492
Ⓜ Barberini
Opening hours: 10 a.m.–1 p.m., 3–6 p.m., Mon–Fri; 10 a.m.–1 p.m., Saturday and Sunday

This church is situated at the junction of Strada Felice, opened by Pope Sixtus V in 1586, and Strada Pia, which Pope Pius IV had construted in 1565. In 1634 Borromini was commissioned to build a monastery and church for the Spanish Discalced Trinitarians. He first built the cloisters, then the church, dedicated to the Holy Trinity and St. Charles Borromeo, and now better known as San Carlino alle Quattro Fontane. In 1664 work began on the celebrated façade, finished after Borromini's death in 1667 by his nephew Bernardo. The great architect

brilliantly solved the problems of having to work on a restricted site and place his building at the junction between two streets. The façade is closely integrated with the convent, which continues beyond the corner, giving an unusual diagonal view of the church which includes the façade, the convent and the fountain on the corner, with its pointed campanile. The façade is on two superimposed levels, curved in the shape of a double S, convex in the center and concave on the two wings. Above the doorway is a niche, crowned by a tympanum formed of the outspread wings of two angels. On the upper part is a rich, curving pavilion on a small balcony flanked by four columns aligned with those below, terminating in a tilted oval lucarne supported by two flying angels. The lantern of the elliptical dome is made up of four concave niches separated by small

columns. The interior, on an elliptical plan, with its major axis lengthways, also creates a sense of contraction, as against expansion. The single order of columns deliberately creates a sense of disproportion in a space whose surfaces are forced to curve. The dome, squeezed and distorted by the tangential curves of the arches, is decorated with octagonal, hexagonal and cruciform coffers. A chapel in the crypt was set aside for Borromini, who committed suicide in 1667, but it has always been empty.

④ SANTA MARIA DELLA VITTORIA

Via XX Settembre, 17
📞 06 42 74 05 71
🚌 60, 61, 62, 84, 492, 910
Ⓜ Repubblica
Opening hours: 9 a.m.–12 p.m., 3:30–6:30 p.m. Mon–Sat; 3:30–6 p.m. Sun

The church is especially famous for Gian Lorenzo Bernini's masterpiece, the *Ecstasy of St. Teresa*, completed in 1646 and placed in the Cornaro Chapel. In an almost theatrical setting, the donor, Cardinal Francesco Cornaro, and his family witness the saint's ecstasy, as she lies on a cloud, her mouth and eyes half closed. In front of her, an angel holding a dart is about to pierce her heart,

according to a passage
recounted in the *Life of
St. Teresa*. This altarpiece
demonstrates Bernini's
innovation in handling
his subject: the viewer
is an involuntary witness
of the extraordinary
event. Scenes from the
life of the saint of Avila
are depicted on the vault
in gilded stucco relief.
The Victory to which the
name of the church refers
is that won in 1620 by
Ferdinand II Habsburg,
thanks to a miraculous
image of Mary found
in Bohemia. The church
was therefore built in
the first half of the 17th
century; it was designed
by Carlo Maderno.
The interior shows its
Baroque style, with its
rich marble and the
ornamentation of its
single nave and six side
chapels. Visible in one
of them are the last
canvases painted in Rome
by Domenichino, The
Ecstasy of St. Francis and
*St. Francis Receiving the
Stigmata*, dated to 1630.
In the third chapel
on the left is Guercino's
Holy Trinity, painted
around 1642.

㊷ SANTA MARIA DEGLI ANGELI

Piazza della Repubblica
☎ 06 48 80 812
🚌 36, 60, 61, 62, 64, 84,
90, 116, 170, 1/3, 492, 910
Ⓜ Repubblica
Opening hours: 7 a.m.–
6:30 p.m.

Giuliano da Sangallo and
Baldassarre Peruzzi had
already had the idea of
transforming the Baths of
Diocletian but it was not
until 1561, under Pius
IV, that the rooms of the
baths were consecrated
to the angels and the
Christian martyrs who
according to legend helped
to build the Roman
complex. Michelangelo
was commissioned to
carry out the project,
and produced a building
that was almost a Greek
cross. Further alterations
in the 18th century
were completed by Luigi
Vanvitelli for the Holy
Year of 1750, giving the
basilica its present form.
The 16th-century façade
was demolished in the
20th century so as to
expose the Roman walls.

In the vestibule, converted
from the old calidarium
or hot room, are the
funerary monuments of
the painters Carlo Maratta
and Salvator Rosa, and of
Cardinal Francesco Alciati,
by Giovanni Battista Della
Porta. The transverse nave
is formed from the old
tepidarium, or cool room,
covered by three groin-
vaults on huge monolithic
granite columns.
In the sanctuary is
Domenichino's *Martyrdom
of St. Sebastian* (1629)
and Giovanni Francesco
Romanelli's *Presentation
of Mary in the Temple*
(1640).

㊸ SANTA PRASSEDE

Via di Santa Prassede, 9/a
☎ 06 48 82 456
Ⓜ Cavour
🚌 16, 70, 71, 75, 714
Opening hours: 7:30
a.m.–12 p.m., 4–6:30
p.m. (only in the
afternoon in August)

This was an old *titulus*
(parish church) dating
back at least to the 5th
century and dedicated to
the figure of Praxedes, who

according to tradition was the sister of Pudentiana and daughter of the senator Pudens, who is said to have hosted St. Paul. Today very little remains of the early Christian church, which

was completely rebuilt by Pope Paschal I (817–824), who transferred to it from the catacombs the remains of about two thousand martyrs. Further changes and additions were made in the 16th century, and the sanctuary area and the crypt were rebuilt in the 18th century. The magnificent 9th-century mosaic in the apse shows, below the monogram of Paschal I, the Saviour with Sts. Peter and Paul, Pudentiana and Praxedes, St. Zeno, and the Pope as donor. Below, the Mystical Lamb on the mountain of Paradise is surrounded by twelve sheep, symbolizing the Apostles, who are leaving Jerusalem and Bethlehem. The triumphal arch and the arch of the apse are decorated with other mosaics of the same period. The right-

hand nave leads to the cruciform Chapel of San Zeno, covered in mosaics, and a veritable gem of Byzantine art in Rome. It was dedicated by Paschal I to his mother, Theodora, who is buried here. In a small side room is the pillar of the scourging, brought from Jerusalem in 1223, and considered a relic of Christ's Passion.

44 SAN PIETRO IN VINCOLI

Piazza San Pietro in Vincoli, 4/a
📞 06 97 84 49 50
🚌 75, 84, 117
Ⓜ Cavour, Colosseo
Opening hours: 8 a.m.–12:30 p.m., 3–7 p.m. (Oct–Mar 6 p.m.)

The church also known as the "basilica Eudoxiana," and it rises up on the ruins of an Imperial villa, on which Eudoxia, wife of the Emperor Valentinian III, had a basilica built in the 5th century as a place to keep the chains in which St. Peter was held captive in Jerusalem. Legend has it that they were

miraculously welded with those used to imprison the saint in the Mamertine prison in Rome, which are now preserved under the 19th-century high altar. The church was consecrated by Pope Sixtus III (432–440), restored by Adrian I (772–795) and consolidated in the 11th century, after the Norman invasion. Between 1471 and 1503, the future Pope Julius II, Cardinal Giuliano della Rovere, had the side naves and transept covered by a groin-vault, and the portico entirely reconstructed. It was raised in the 17th century, hiding the old façade, and is now altered by the modern Via Cavour. The interior has three naves, with a 17th-century fresco by Parodi on the ceiling of the central one. Other features include a 7th-century Byzantine mosaic representing *St. Sebastian*, a *Deposition of Christ* by Pomarancio, in the first altar in the left-hand nave, and paintings by Guercino and Domenichino in the right-hand nave. The most famous work of art is

Michelangelo's *Moses*, part of the proposed memorial of Julius II, an awe-inspiring work intended for St. Peter's in the Vatican. This statue is extraordinarily powerful, exuding superhuman energy and strength of character, in keeping with the sculptor's vehement and passionate nature.

④⑤ SANTI QUATTRO CORONATI

Via dei Santi Quattro, 20
📞 06 70 47 54 20
🚌 85, 117, 850
🚊 3
Ⓜ Colosseo
Opening hours: 6:30 a.m.–12:30 p.m., 3:30–7:45 p.m.

The church was founded by Pope Melchiades (311–314) to honor the Four Crowned Martyrs, Severus, Severianus, Carpophorus and Victorinus, who refused to worship an idol of the god Aesculapius. It is also dedicated to the five Pannonian stone-cutters who declined a request to carve the idol. Pope Leo IV (625–638) brought their relics to the church. Honorius I (625–638) restored it, but it was destroyed in the sack of Rome by the Normans in 1084 and restored again by Pope Paschal II (1099–1118), who created three naves from the single central one. The left-hand nave was then demolished to make way for the cloisters, and the right-hand one turned into a refectory. In 1521 the church, administered by the Benedictines since the 12th century, passed into the hands of the Camaldolese and in 1560 to the Augustinians, who are still responsible for it. The complex resembles a kind of "fortified convent," a defensive bastion for San Giovanni in Laterano. In fact, it stands on the edge of the route of the papal procession from the Lateran to the Vatican. The apse closes off the three naves, since it is part of the old church; it has a fresco by Giovanni da San Giovanni. The skull of St. Sebastian is preserved in the left-hand altar. A door in the left-hand nave leads to the Romanesque cloisters. Located in the Chapel of San Silvestro are frescoes of 1246, depicting Scenes from the *Life of the Saint* and the *Legend of Constantine*, and in the portico between the two courtyards there is one of the *Last Judgement*.

④⑥ SANCTUARY OF THE MADONNA DEL DIVINO AMORE

🚌 218 from San Giovanni in Laterano, 702 from P.le Ostiense.
Opening hours: 6:30 a.m.–8 p.m.

"Rome's new Marian Sanctuary, alongside its oldest, Santa Maria Maggiore" is how John Paul II described this shrine. Since 1740, the year when the first miracle took place, pilgrims have been coming here to renew their faith, calling on the intercession of the Virgin Mary. To ward off the city's destruction during World War II, Romans made a votive offering at the shrine. It has been included in the official itinerary for pilgrims in Holy Year, and is a place where they obtain indulgences.

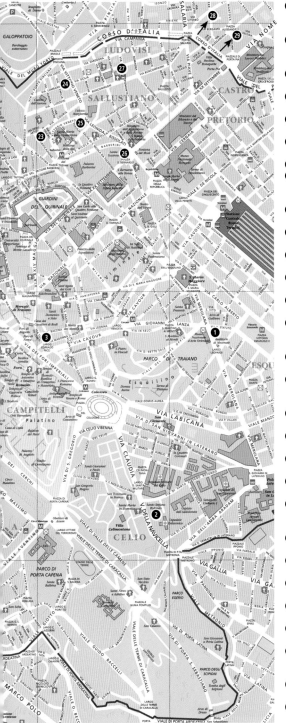

28 Nostra Signora del Santissimo Sacramento e Santi Martiri Canadesi (Canada)

8 Nostra Signora di Guadalupe e San Filippo martire in via Aurelia (Mexico)

12 San Giosafat al Gianicolo (Ukraine)

24 San giovanni Marone (Lebanon) Syrian-maronite rite

20 San Girolamo dei Croati (Croatia)

6 San Giuliano dei Fiamminghi (Belgium)

16 San Luigi dei Francesi (France)

25 San Nicola daTolentino agli Orti Sallustiani (Armenia) Armenian rite

27 San Patrizio a Villa Ludovisi (Ireland)

18 San Salvatore alle Coppelle (Rumania) Byzantine-rumanian rite

22 San Silvestro in Capite (England)

5 San Stanislao alle Botteghe Oscure (Poland)

14 San Tommaso in Parione (Ethiopia) coptic rite

1 Sant'Antonio abate all'Esquilino (Russia) Byzantine-russian rite

17 Sant'Antonio in Campo Marzio (Portugal)

21 Sant'Atanasio a via del Babuino (Greece) Byzantine-greek rite

23 Sant'Isidoro a Capo le Case (Ireland)

7 Santa Brigida a Campo de' Fiori (Sweden)

29 Santa Maria Addolorata a piazza Buenos Aires (Argentina)

15 Santa Maria dell'Anima (Germany)

19 Santa Maria della Concezione in Campo Marzio (Syria) syrian-antiochene rite

4 Santa Maria in Cosmedin Byzantine-greek-melchite rite

13 Santa Maria in Monserrato degli Spagnoli (Spain)

9 Santa Sofia (Ukraine) Byzantine-ukrainian rite

26 Santa Susanna alle Terme di Diocleziano (United States)

11 Santi Michele e Magno (Netherlands)

3 Santi Sergio e Bacco o Madonna del Pascolo (Ukraine) byzantine-ukrainian rite

10 Santo Stefano degli Abissini (Ethiopia) coptic rite

2 Santo Stefano Rotondo al Celio (Hungary)

❶ SANT'ANTONIO ABATE ALL'ESQUILINO

(Russia)
Byzantine-russian rite

Via Carlo Alberto, 2
☎ 06 44 86 98 58
🚌 4, 70, 71
Ⓜ Vittorio Emanuele
Closed: July and August

In 1259 Cardinal Pietro Capocci had a hospital built near the early Christian church of Sant'Andrea Cata Barbara (or in Piscinula), which had been erected in the 5th century on the site of the pagan residence of Julius Bassus (4th century). The hospital was named after the church, and in 1289 the name San Giovanni di Gerusalemme agli Antoniani was added. The lovely Romanesque doorway by the Vassalletto family, facing Via Carlo Alberto, is a remnant of the medieval building. In 1308 the Antonines founded a new church, dedicated to St. Antony Abbot, which

underwent many modifications over the centuries. Inside, the frescoes by Pomarancio and the chapel of Sant'Antonio are of interest. By the end of the 16h century, the buildings had been surrounded by a wall, and the old Church of Sant'Andrea had fallen into ruin. The church acquired its present appearance in the early 1700s. On January 17, the feast day of St. Anthony, considered the patron saint of animals, horses and carts would be solemnly blessed outside it. In 1928 the Holy See acquired the whole site in order to build four pontifical institutes, and the church was included in one of them, the Pontifical Institute Russicum. In 1932 it was handed over to Russian Catholics of the Byzantine-Slavonic rite and the interior was slightly altered to create an iconostasis and adapt it to the Byzantine liturgy.

❷ SANTO STEFANO ROTONDO AL CELIO

(Hungary)

Via di Santo Stefano Rotondo, 7
(See p. 137)

❸ SANTI SERGIO E BACCO O MADONNA DEL PASCOLO (Ukraine)

byzantine-ukrainian rite

Piazza Madonna dei Monti, 3
🚌 115
Ⓜ Cavour

The Ukrainian church is situated in the heart of the city's Monti quarter. It is recorded as early as the 9th century and owes its present form to its reconstruction by the 18th-century architect Francesco Ferrari. The façade is dated to 1896.

❹ SANTA MARIA IN COSMEDIN

Byzantine-greek-melchite rite

Piazza Bocca della Verità 18
(See p. 136)

❺ SAN STANISLAO ALLE BOTTEGHE OSCURE

(Poland)

Via delle Botteghe Oscure, 15
☎ 06 67 95 347
🚌 44, 46, 170, 186

The first church on this site was dedicated to the San Salvatore Pensilis de Surraca, and was already mentioned in a document of 1174. In 1582, Gregory XIII granted it

to the Polish Cardinal Stanislaus Hosius, who rebuilt it and dedicated it to St. Stanislas, Bishop of Krakow, martyred in 1079 and Poland's patron saint. The Polish church, with its attached hospice, was completely rebuilt in 1753.

❻ San Giuliano dei Fiamminghi (Belgium)

Via del Sudario, 40
☎ 06 68 72 550
🚌 8, 44, 64, 70, 115

Tradition has it that this little church was founded when Flanders converted to the faith, during the papacy of Gregory II (715–753). It is known for its wonderful Baroque façade. Above the façade door is a statue of St. Julian the Hospitaller, a saint of unknown nationality adopted by the Belgians as their patron and believed to come from Ath, in Hainaut.

❼ Santa Brigida a Campo de' Fiori (Sweden)

Piazza Farnese, 96
☎ 06 68 89 25 96
🚌 62, 64, 116

The oldest church goes back to the time of Boniface IX (1389–1404). It was left abandoned until Pope Paul III (1534–1549) assigned it to the Bishop of Uppsala, Olaus Magnus. Along with its hospice, it was

later handed over to the Convertite sisters. It was totally restored in the 18th century.

❽ Nostra Signora di Guadalupe e San Filippo martire in via Aurelia (Mexico)

Via Aurelia 675
☎ 06 66 41 17 30
🚌 246

This parish church was built in 1960 and is cared for by the Missionaries of the Sacred Heart of Jesus (Legionaries of Christ).

❾ Santa Sofia (Ukraine)
Byzantine-ukrainian rite
Via Boccea 478
☎ 06 62 40 203
🚌 904, 905, 906

When Cardinal Josyf Slipyj, Metropolitan of the Ukrainian Catholic Church, returned from his twenty-year exile in Siberia, he had this church built between 1967 and 1968. It is called the Sober (meaning Mother

Church) or meeting place for special festivals, of Holy Wisdom, and is the spiritual and religious center for all Ukrainians. On September 28, 1976, Pope Paul VI brought the relics of Pope St. Clement (88–97) to the church. The church boasts a beautiful iconostasis, painted by Juvenalij Josyf Mokryckyj.

❿ Santo Stefano degli Abissini (Ethiopia)
coptic rite

Città del Vaticano
🚌 904, 905, 906

Pope Leo III (795–816) had this church built and named it for St. Stephen the Greater. In 1479 it was assigned by Sixtus IV to the Coptic monks. Under Clement XI (1700–1721) it was radically altered. It has a notable doorway, with the Lamb and the cross (12th century).

11 SANTI MICHELE E MAGNO
(Netherlands)

Borgo Santo Spirito
☏ 06 70 05 745
🚍 62, 810, 982
Ⓜ Ottaviano, San Pietro

This church, known in the Netherlands as "Church of the Friesians," was, in the Middle Ages, part of the "School of the Friesians," where pilgrims coming to Rome from Holland gathered. The present church dates from 1141 and was restored in 1756. From the 15th century it belonged to the Fabric of St. Peter's and was entrusted to the Archconfraternity of the Most Holy Sacrament. Since 1989 the Dutch community has used the church on Sundays.

12 SAN GIOSAFAT AL GIANICOLO
(Ukraine)

Passeggiata del Gianicolo, 4
🚍 870

This church is annexed to the Pontifical Ukrainian College of St. Josaphat, founded in 1897.

13 SANTA MARIA IN MONSERRATO DEGLI SPAGNOLI (Spain)

Via Giulia, 151
☏ 06 68 89 651
🚍 116

Built in 1518, to designs by Antonio da Sangallo the Younger, with a façade made up of pilaster strips by Francesco da Volterra, it rise up on the site of a complex belonging to the Catalans. Alexander VI Borgia (1492–1503) established a Spanish national fraternity in the church, under the protection of the Virgin of Montserrat. The church contains the tombs of the Borgia Popes Callixtus III (1455–1458) and Alexander VI, which were removed from St. Peter's when the new basilica was built. A room next to the church contains a portrait of Cardinal Pedro Montoya, one of Gian Lorenzo Bernini's earliest works.

14 SAN TOMMASO IN PARIONE
(Ethiopia) Coptic rite

Via del Parione, 33
🚍 46, 62, 64, 70, 81, 87, 115, 492, 628

The church was consecrated by Pope Innocent II in 1139, and rebuilt in 1582 to a design by Francesco da Volterra.

15 SANTA MARIA DELL'ANIMA
(Germany)

Via Santa Maria dell'Anima, 64
☏ 06 68 28 18 02
🚍 46, 62, 64, 70, 81, 87, 115, 492, 628

The church rises up on the site of the chapel of the hospice for pilgrims from Germany and the Netherlands. It was rebuilt in the early 16th century. Its fine façade is attributed to Giuliano da Sangallo. The three doors, and the *Madonna and Two Souls*, which gives the church its name, have recently been attributed to Sansovino. The church was completely restored in 1843. It contains many works of art from different periods, by Italian, Flemish and German artists. Of special interest is Giulio Romano's *The Holy Family and Saints* (1522).

16 SAN LUIGI DEI FRANCESI (France)

Piazza San Luigi dei Francesi, 5
(See p. 149)

**⓱ SANT'ANTONIO
IN CAMPO MARZIO
(Portugal)**

Via dei Portoghesi, 2
☏ 06 68 80 24 96
🚌 46

The earliest church,
dating back to 1440,
was built by Cardinal
Martin de Chavez in a
predominantly Portuguese
quarter. It was rebuilt
in 1630, with an ornate
Baroque façade by
Martino Longhi the
Younger. The polychrome
interior is by Carlo
Rainaldi and Cristoforo
Schor. The monument
of Alexander de Souza,
by Antonio Canova, and
the paintings by Nicolas
Lorrain and Antoniazzo
Romano are of interest.

**⓲ SAN SALVATORE
ALLE COPPELLE
(Rumania)**
Byzantine-rumanian rite

Piazza delle Coppelle,
72/b
Tel.: 06 68 92 929
🚌 116

The church is dated to
before 1195, based on

an inscription inside that
mentions Celestine III
(1190-1198); it was under
his reign that the bell-tower
was built. The church was
rebuilt in 1700.

**⓳ SANTA MARIA DELLA
CONCEZIONE IN
CAMPO MARZIO
(Syria)**
syrian-antiochene rite

Piazza Campo Marzio, 45
🚌 81, 115, 116, 117,
492, 628

Pious legend would
have us believe that the
nuns of the convent
of St. Anastasia in
Constantinople fled to
Rome in 750 to escape
persecution by the
iconoclasts under the
Emperors Leo III and
Constantine V, bringing
with them the body of
St. Gregory Nazianzene.
In Rome, Pope Zacharias
is said to have had a
convent built for them
in the Campus Martius,
where they built two
churches, one dedicated
to Mary, the other to St.
Gregory Nazianzene. The
church of Santa Maria
della Concezione was first

enlarged by Giacomo della
Porta in 1564, and again,
in its entirety, by Giovanni
Antonio De Rossi, in
1685. Inside it features a
Greek cross plan, with a
dome. Over the high altar
is a painting dating from
the 12th or 13th century,
representing the Virgin as
Advocate.

**⓴ SAN GIROLAMO
DEI CROATI (Croatia)**

Via Tomacelli, 132
☏ 06 99 69 44 10
🚌 81, 115, 628, 926
Ⓜ Spagna

When the Turks invaded
Illyria, many people
fled and took refuge in
Rome, possibly in the area
where the church of San
Girolamo was built later.
In 1453, Pope Nicholas V
gave them the land they
needed to build a hospice.
The church was rebuilt
under Sixtus V by Martino
Longhi the Elder.

**㉑ SANT'ATANASIO
A VIA DEL BABUINO
(Greece)**
Byzantine-greek rite

Via del Babuino 149
☏ 06 36 00 12 61
🚌 117

The church was built
by Giacomo della Porta
during the papacy of
Gregory XIII (1572–
1585), when the Greek
College was founded. It
has a brick façade with
two bell-towers. The high
altar, in accordance with
the Greek rite, is cut off

by the wooden iconostasis by Andrea Busiri Vici (1876), which replaced an earlier one. In the apse is a *Crucifixion* by the Cavalier d'Arpino.

㉒ SAN SILVESTRO IN CAPITE (England)

Piazza San Silvestro
📞 06 69 77 121
🚌 52, 53, 58, 58 barr., 71, 85, 160, 850

Paul I (757–767) built a monastery, dedicated to Popes St. Sylvester and St. Stephen, on the site of the pagan temple of the Sun. The two saints were buried in the adjoining oratory. The complex was called *inter duos hortos,* and also *in capite,* because relics of the head of John the Baptist were kept there. The church was rebuilt in 1198, when the lovely bell-tower was added. It acquired its present form between the late 16th and early 18th centuries, from artists such as Francesco da Volterra, Carlo

Maderno, Carlo Rainaldi, Mattia and Domenico De Rossi. Its notable works of art include a painting by Orazio Gentileschi and frescoes in the dome by Pomarancio and his collaborators.

㉓ SANT'ISIDORO A CAPO LE CASE (Ireland)

Via degli Artisti, 41
📞 06 48 85 359
Ⓜ Barberini
🚌 52, 53, 56, 58, 58 barr., 95

The church and its adjoining college were founded by Ottaviano Vestri di Barbiano, after a papal Bull of Urban VIII in 1525, and entrusted to Irish Reformed Observant Franciscans. The portico and façade are by Bizzacheri (1704). The church contains paintings by Maratta and some architectural features and sculpture attributed to Bernini. Next to the church is the lovely aula

maxima or main hall of Luke Wadding's college, with important fresco cycles by Fra Emanuele da Como. This was the scene of the famous disputes of the "Scotist" followers of the philosopher-theologian Duns Scotus (circa 1266–1308).

㉔ SAN GIOVANNI MARONE (Lebanon) Syrian-maronite rite

Via Aurora, 6
🚌 95, 116

The church, built in 1924, is annexed to the Maronite College.

㉕ SAN NICOLA DA TOLENTINO AGLI ORTI SALLUSTIANI (Armenia) Armenian rite

Salita di San Nicola da Tolentino, 17
📞 06 42 45 801
Ⓜ Barberini

Built in 1599, at the behest of Prince Camillo Pamphilj, it was rebuilt in 1614 by the architect Giovanni Maria Baratta. Its Baroque façade, with steps in front, is of

particular interest. It is annexed to the Pontifical Armenian College.

㉖ SANTA SUSANNA ALLE TERME DI DIOCLEZIANO
(United States)

Via XX Settembre 14
📞 06 48 82 748
🚌 16, 37, 60, 61, 62, 136, 137

The church has gone through numerous phases of development, from ancient times to the 17th century. One of the legends is that it was where St. Susanna was martyred, and the *titulus* of Pope Caius (283–296), brother of Gabinus, her father. Pope Leo III (795–816) had the oldest phase (possibly a large 4th-century church with an apse and internal galleries) decorated with mosaics. It was rebuilt under Sixtus IV, and then by Cardinal Rusticucci between 1593 and 1603, when it was completed by Carlo Maderno.

㉗ SAN PATRIZIO A VILLA LUDOVISI
(Ireland)

Via Boncompagni 31
📞 06 42 03 12 01
🚌 52, 53, 56, 58, 58 barr., 95
Ⓜ Barberini

Built in the early 1900s in the Nordic Neo-romantic style, to a design by Aristide Leonori. It contains frescoes from the old church of Santa Maria in Posterula, which was demolished when San Patrizio was built.

㉘ NOSTRA SIGNORA DEL SANTISSIMO SACRAMENTO E SANTI MARTIRI CANADESI
(Canada)

Via Giovanni Battista de Rossi, 46
📞 06 44 23 79 84
🚌 9, 490, 495
Ⓜ Policlinico

In 1948 the Generalate of the Blessed Sacrament Fathers acquired a piece of land on which to build a center, and a parish church was added later. Because

Canada had helped to pay for it to be built, it was dedicated to the Martyrs of Canada (1630–1680). The unusually bold architecture is the work of Bruno Apollonj Ghetti (1955) while the internal furnishings and decoration are by contemporary artists.

㉙ SANTA MARIA ADDOLORATA A PIAZZA BUENOS AIRES
(Argentina)

Viale Regina Margherita, 81
📞 06 84 40 13 01
🚌 19, 30

Monsignor José Leon Gallardo laid the first stone of the church of Santa Maria Addolorata on July 9, 1910, the centenary of Argentina's independence. Benedict XV made it the Argentine national church in 1915, and it is administered by the Argentine Bishops' Conference.

REGIONAL CHURCHES

ABRUZZI
Santa Maria Maddalena
in Campo Marzio
Piazza della Maddalena,
56

BERGAMO
Santi Bartolomeo e
Alessandro a Piazza
Colonna
Via di Pietra, 70

BOLOGNA
Santi Giovanni
Evangelista e Petronio
dei Bolognesi
Via del Mascherone, 61

CALABRIA
San Francesco di Paola
ai Monti
Piazza San Francesco di
Paola, 10

FLORENCE
San Giovanni Battista
de' Fiorentini
Via Acciaioli, 2

GENOA
San Giovanni Battista dei
Genovesi
Via Anicia, 12

LOMBARDY
Santi Ambrogio e Carlo
al Corso
Via del Corso, 240

LUCCA
Santa Croce e San
Bonaventura alla Pilotta
Via dei Lucchesi, 3

NAPLES
Santo Spirito
dei Napoletani
Via Giulia, 34

NICE
See Piedmont

NORCIA
Santi Benedetto e
Scolastica
Vicolo Sinibaldi, 1

**PICENO AND
MARCHE**
San Salvatore in Lauro
Piazza San Salvatore in
Lauro, 15

PIEDMONT
Santissimo Sudario
all'Argentina
Via del Sudario, 47

APULIA
San Nicola in Carcere
Via del Teatro Marcello,
46

SIENA
Santa Caterina da Siena
a Via Giulia
Via Monserrato, 111

SICILY
Santa Maria Odigitria al
Tritone
Via Anicia, 12

VENICE
San Marco Evangelista
al Campidoglio
Piazza San Marco, 48

HOMES
OF THE SAINTS

22 Blessed Josephine Vannini
1 St. Agnes
27 St. Aloysius Gonzaga
2 St. Augustine and St. Monica
4 St. Benedict Joseph Labre
3 St. Benedict of Nursia
5 St. Bridget of Sweden
6 St. Camillus de Lellis
8 St. Catherine of Siena
9 St. Cecilia
7 St. Charles of Sezze
10 St. Dominic of Guzman
11 St. Felix of Cantalice
   and St. Crispino of Viterbo
13 St. Frances of Rome
14 St. Francis of Assisi
23 St. Gregory the Great
24 St. Ignatius Loyola
16 St. John-Baptist De Rossi
17 St. John Berchmans
18 St. John Bosco
19 St. John Calabytes
20 St. John of Matha
21 St. Joseph Calasanctius
25 St. Leonard of Porto
   Maurizio
28 St. Madeleine Sophie Barat
29 St. Paola Frassinetti
30 St. Paul
31 St. Paul of the Cross
32 St. Peter
31 St. Philip Neri
33 St. Stanislaus Kostka
34 St. Vincent Pallotti
15 Sts. John and Paul

❶ ST. AGNES

Via Nomentana, 349
☎ 06 86 10 840
🚌 36, 60, 84, 90
Opening hours: 7:30
a.m.–12 p.m., 4–7:45
p.m.

It is traditionally believed
that the family home
of St. Agnes (d. Rome,
3rd century), rose up in
the area that is currently
occupied by the Almo
Collegio Capranica (Piazza
Capranica 98), where she
is venerated as the patron
of the college in a chapel
dedicated to her. The
place of her martyrdom is
traditionally identified as
the underground area of
the church of Sant'Agnese
in Agone near Piazza
Navona (Via Santa Maria
dell'Anima 30). The
church of Sant'Agnese
fuori le Mura contains this
Roman saint's tomb.

❷ ST. AUGUSTINE AND ST. MONICA

Piazza di Santa Monica, 1
Lido di Ostia
☎ 06 56 91 285
🚉 Stazione Ostiense

Augustine and his mother
Monica (4th century)
travelled through Rome
on their way back to
Africa. In his *Confessions*
the saint describes the
ecstasy he and his mother
experienced at a house
in Ostia Tiberina while
waiting to board their
ship (Confessions, 9,
10, 23–26). A plaque in
the archaeological site at

Ostia, close to the Roman
Theatre, records this
event.

❸ ST. BENEDICT OF NURSIA

Piazza in Piscinula, 40
☎ 06 39 03 05 17
🚌 23, 717, 774, 780

The small church of San
Benedetto in Piscinula
rises up on the ruins of
an ancient domus that
belonged to the family of
St. Benedict (Norcia 480–
Cassino 547). It is believed
that the saint lived here
after leaving Norcia in
497. From the vestibule,
a large doorway leads to
the "cell" where the saint
is believed to have studied
and prayed.

❹ ST. BENEDICT JOSEPH LABRE

Via dei Serpenti, 2
🚌 115

On the first floor of this
house, the two rooms
where the saint (St.
Sulpice d'Amette, France,
1748–Rome 1783) spent
the last two years of his life
and where his *memorabilia*
are preserved, are open to
visitors.

❺ ST BRIDGET OF SWEDEN

Piazza Farnese, 96
☎ 06 68 89 25 96
🚌 62, 64, 116

The founder of the
Augustinian Order of the
Saviour, known as the

"brigidine" (Brigittines)
(Finsta, Sweden, 1303–
Rome 1373), lived in a
house on the site where
the church of Santa
Brigida now stands. The
rooms on the second
floor of the adjoining
monastery, where the saint
lived for four years, and
where she died in 1358,
are open to visitors.

❻ ST. CAMILLUS DE LELLIS

Piazza della Maddalena, 53
🚌 116

In 1571, before taking
his vows, St. Camillus
(Bucchianico di Chieti
1550–Rome 1614) went
to work in the hospital of
San Giacomo in Augusta
(Via Canova, 29), where
he slowly made the
decision to convert and
to devote his life to the
sick and the suffering.
He later returned there
to begin to write the
Rule of the Order of the
Ministers to the Sick.
In 1586 the founder of
the "Camilliani" and his
brethren moved to the
church of Santa Maria
Maddalena in Campus
Martius, where the order's
mother-house was built.
The infirmary and the
rooms where Camillus
lived are open to the
public and the room
where he died is now a
chapel containing his
remains.

❼ St Charles of Sezze

Piazza San Francesco d'Assisi, 88
C 06 58 19 020
🚌 8

From 1646 to 1648, brother Charles (Sezze 1613–Rome 1670) lived in the convent of San Pietro in Montorio (Piazza San Pietro in Montorio, 2). In 1648 he received the eucharistic stigmata in the church of San Giuseppe a Capo le Case (Via Francesco Crispi). By then seriously ill, he moved to the infirmary of the convent of San Francesco d'Assisi at Ripa Grande, where he died in 1670. The convent has a small museum where his relics and *memorabilia* are preserved.

❽ St. Catherine of Siena

Piazza Santa Chiara, 14
🚌 116

Summoned by Urban VI, Catherine (Siena 1347–Rome 1380) arrived in Rome on November 28, 1378 with a group of disciples, and lived there until her death. She fought against schism, and wrote many letters in support of the legitimate Pope. Her daily pilgrimage to St. Peter's took its toll on her strength. The room where she died was turned into a chapel in the 17th century. Its wooden ceiling has survived intact, and its old

walls form a votive chapel, accessible from Santa Maria sopra Minerva.

❾ St. Cecilia

Piazza Santa Cecilia, 22
C 06 45 49 27 39
🚋 H, 23
🚌 8
Opening hours: 9:15 a.m.–12:45 p.m., 4–6 p.m.

Beneath the Church of Santa Cecilia in Trastevere are the remains of a Roman house which is believed to have been the home of St. Cecilia (d. Rome, 3rd century). In a side chapel to the left there are traces of a calidarium (bathroom), perhaps the one where she was suffocated.

❿ St. Dominic Guzman

Piazzale Numa Pompilio, 8
🚌 628, 714

St. Dominic (Caleruega, Spain 1175–1221) visited Rome on many occasions. From late 1220 to early 1221 he lived in the convent of San Sisto Vecchio on the Appian Way, a gift of Pope Honorius III after he recognized the Dominican order. In 1221 he lived in the convent of Santa Sabina all'Aventino (Piazza Pietro d'Illiria, 1), where his room was turned into a venerated chapel by Pope Clement IX.

⓫ St. Felix of Cantalice and St. Crispin of Viterbo

Via Veneto, 27
Ⓜ Barberini

The small cells of St. Felix (Cantalice 1515–Rome 1587) and St. Crispin (Viterbo 1668–Rome 1750), places of devotion for the faithful and for Popes, have been reconstructed behind the choir in the church of the Immacolata Concezione.

⓬ St. Philip Neri

Via del Governo Vecchio, 134
🚌 46, 62, 64

From 1551 to 1583, St. Philip (Florence 1515–Rome 1595) lived in the house (now the Sanctuary Filippino) adjacent to the church of San Girolamo della Carità (Via Monserrato 62/A), where he started his apostolate and founded the Oratory. The "Rooms of St. Philip Neri," with many paintings representing incidents and miracles associated with him, can be reached from the sacristy. During the 1575 Jubilee, Philip welcomed poor pilgrims at the oratory of the Santissima Trinità dei Pellegrini (Via dei Pettinari 36/A), and led the cardinals and Roman noblemen who assisted them. In 1575 Gregory XIII gave Philip the small church of Santa Maria in Vallicella. The saint had it rebuilt (it is now known as the Chiesa Nuova, or "New Church"), and also built the nearby oratory of the Philippines. The urn containing his remains is preserved inside the church, in the chapel named after him. The "Rooms of St. Philip Neri" where the saint lived and died can be visited.

⑬ ST. FRANCES OF ROME

Via Teatro di Marcello, 32
☎ 06 67 97 135
Ⓜ Colosseo
🚌 85, 87, 115, 170, 492

For most of her life, Frances (Rome 1384–Rome 1440) lived in her husband's palace, the Palazzo Ponziani (in the Trastevere area). She founded the order of the Oblates of Monteoliveto, and after being widowed, joined the sisters in 1436 in the monastery of the house of the noble Oblates of Tor de' Specchi (Via del Teatro di Marcello, 32). This is where she spent the last years of her life, and the "Rooms of St. Frances of Rome" are to be found. Her remains are venerated in the church of Santa Francesca Romana on the Palatine hill (formerly Santa Maria Nuova).

⑭ ST. FRANCIS OF ASSISI

Piazza San Francesco d'Assisi, 88
☎ 06 58 19 020
🚌 8

The church of San Francesco d'Assisi a Ripa was the main residence of St. Francis (Assisi 1182–Assisi 1226) in Rome. The place where he used to pray can be reached from the sacristy. On the right-hand wall is the stone pillow where the saint would lay his head during his hours of rest. In the courtyard of the convent is a bitter-orange tree, known as a melangolo, planted by Francis himself.

⑮ STS. JOHN AND PAUL

Piazza dei Santi Giovanni e Paolo, 13
☎ 06 77 27 11
🚌 117

The church of Santi Giovanni e Paolo al Celio rises up on the site of their family home, where the two martyrs, who died in Rome in 362, during the persecutions of Julian the Apostate, were secretly buried. The exact location of their house and the place of their martyrdom is marked on the floor of the church.

⑯ ST. JOHN-BAPTIST DE ROSSI

Piazza Bocca della verità, 18
☎ 06 67 81 415
🚌 23, 44, 81, 95, 160, 170, 175, 280, 628, 715, 716

Hardly anything remains of the places where St. John-Baptist (Voltaggio–Rome 1764) once lived. The hospice of Santa Galla, where he carried out his ministry, was demolished in 1935; his room in the ecclesiastical college of the Santissima Trinità dei Pellegrini ai Catinari (Via dei Pettinari 36/a) has been completely refurbished, leaving nothing that belonged to him. Only the room in the convent of Santa Maria in Cosmedin where he lived for nine years (between 1751 and 1760) still shows some traces of the saint.

⑰ ST. JOHN BERCHMANS

Via del Caravita, 8/A
☎ 06 67 94 406
🚌 117, 492, 628

St. John (Diest, Belgium 1599–Rome 1621) lived and prayed in the rooms of the Roman College of the Jesuits (Piazza del Collegio Romano, 4), situated between the church of Sant'Ignazio di Loyola and Campus Martius. His room, next to that of St. Aloysius Gonzaga, is venerated, and was turned into a chapel in 1865.

⓲ ST. JOHN BOSCO

Via Marsala, 42
☎ 06 49 27 221
🚌 4, 9, 36, 36 barr., 37, 310, 319, 492

St. John (Becchi, Castelnuovo d'Asti 1815–Turin 1888) visited Rome twenty times, but each time he would stay in a different place each time. He is remembered at the site of his last visit, in May 1887, on the first floor of the Institute adjoining the church of Sacro Cuore di Gesù a Castro Pretorio.

⓳ ST. JOHN CALABYTES

Isola Tiberina, 39
🚌 8, 23, 717, 774, 780

It is believed that the church of San Giovanni Calibita was built on the site of the saint's family home (5th century). When the original church was completely rebuilt, between 1600 and 1700, his body was discovered under the high altar.

⓴ ST. JOHN OF MATHA

Piazza della Navicella, 12
🚌 117

The first seat of the Order of the Trinitarians, founded by St. John of Matha (Fancon, France, 1154–Rome 1213), was the church of San Tommaso in Formis, which can be reached by passing under the Arch of Dolabella at Villa Celimontana park. Inside, the small cell where the saint lived is now venerated. To the left of the church are the remains of the monastery of the Trinitarians.

㉑ ST. JOSEPH CALASANCTIUS

Piazza dei Massimi, 4
🚌 46, 62, 64

Joseph Calasanz (Peralta de la Sal, Spain, 1558–Rome 1648) was the founder of the Piarists. He began teaching poor children in the presbytery of the church of Santa Dorotea (Via Santa Dorotea, 23). In 1612 he built the headquarters of the Piarist order next to the church of San Pantaleo. The room where he lived for 36 years until his death is open to the public.

㉒ BLESSED JOSEPHINE VANNINI
Via Giusti, 7
🚌 16, 85, 186, 714

Josephine Vannini (Rome 1859–Rome 1911), whose baptismal name was Judith, founded, together with Father Luigi Tezza, the Institute of the Daughters of St. Camillus, and was beatified by Pope John Paul II in 1994. This was the first seat of the Institute, leased by the founders on June 78, 1897. It was here that she lived for fourteen years with the first sisters, offering shelter to elderly, sick and deserted women, and it is considered the mother-house. Her body is preserved in the church at the Generalate of the Daughters of St. Camillus at Grottaferrata (Via Anagnina, 18).

㉓ ST. GREGORY THE GREAT

Piazza San Gregorio, 1
☎ 06 70 08 227
🚌 81, 175, 810
Aperto: 9–12, 16–18

St. Gregory (Rome 540–Rome 604) was a Roman nobleman. With the help of other monks he founded a Benedictine community in one of his family's palaces, the Gordian palace on the Caelian hill. He also built a church in honour of the Apostle St. Andrew (now known as the church of Santi Gregorio e Andrea al Celio). In the church, at the back of the nave on the right, is the room where he lived and prayed; it also contains the Bishop's throne. Behind the main church are the three small chapels of St. Andrew, St. Sylvia and St. Barbara. The last of these houses an ancient marble table where, according to tradition, an angel sat down to eat among the twelve poor people fed every day by St. Gregory.

㉔ St. Ignatius Loyola

Piazza del Gesù

☎ 06 69 70 01

🚌 H, 44, 46, 56, 60, 62, 64, 70, 81, 87, 186, 492, 628, 810

St. Ignatius (Loyola, Spain, 1491–Rome 1556) lived in many places in Rome. In 1544 he and the whole Society of Jesus moved to a building next to the old church of Santa Maria della Strada, rebuilt in 1568 and given the new name of Santissimo Nome di Gesù (known as the Church of Gesù). It was the first seat of the Jesuit order. What is left of the old apartment where the saint lived between 1544 and 1556, the "Rooms of St. Ignatius," are open to the public at Piazza del Gesù, 45. The saint's *memorabilia* are preserved in the adjacent rooms.

㉕ St. Leonard of Porto Maurizio

Via San Bonaventura, 4

🚌 85, 87, 175, 186, 850

Ⓜ Colosseo

This saint from Liguria (Porto Maurizio 1676–Rome 1751) spent his noviciate at the Roman College of the Jesuits (Piazza del Collegio Romano, 4), and later went to live in the convent of San Bonaventura al Palatino, where he died in 1751. The room in the infirmary where he died still attracts many visitors and pilgrims.

㉖ St. Lawrence the Martyr

Piazzale del Verano, 3

☎ 06 49 15 11

🚌 71, 492

🚋 19

Opening hours: 7:30 a.m.–12:30 p.m., 4–7 p.m.

A total of thirty-four churches have been devoted to St. Lawrence over the centuries. This saint died in Rome in 257, and each church refers to episodes from his suffering and martyrdom. Together, they are like a "Way of the Cross." According to tradition, the church of San Lorenzo in Lucina (Via in Lucina 16/A) rises up on the remains of the house where he often stayed. Inside the church is the venerated gridiron where he was laid while being tortured. The church of San Lorenzo in Fonte (Via Urbana, 50) marks the place where Lorenzo was jailed. It is believed that the church of San Lorenzo in Panisperna (Via Panisperna, 90) is located on the spot where, lying on the burning metal, he was martyred. The church of San Lorenzo de' Speziali in Miranda (Via in Miranda, 10) is instead located on the spot where he was sentenced. His remains are preserved in the church of San Lorenzo fuori le Mura, and his body was buried in the catacombs of St. Cyriaca, which can be reached via the cloisters there.

㉗ St. Aloysius Gonzaga

Via del Caravita, 8/A

☎ 06 67 94 406

🚌 117, 492, 628

When St. Aloysius (Castiglione delle Stiviere 1568–Rome 1591) arrived in Rome he lived and did his noviciate in study at the Roman College of the Jesuits, now a school (Piazza del Collegio Romano, 4). From inside the church of Sant' Ignazio di Loyola in Campus Martius the visitor can see the room where the saint lived until his death in 1591. After his beatification, the room was turned into an oratory.

㉘ St. Madeleine Sophie Barat

Via San Francesco di Sales, 18

☎ 06 66 80 60 32

🚌 23, 65, 280, 870

St. Madeleine (Soigny, France, 1779–Paris 1865), founder of the Society of the Sacred Heart, arrived in Rome in 1832, and settled with her congregation in the monastery of the church of the Santissima Trinità al Monte Pincio (known as "Trinità dei Monti," Piazza Trinità dei Monti, 39). There she began her mission of educating girls from some of the most prominent Roman families. The order's second house was opened in 1842, with the church of the Sacro Cuore di Gesù at Villa Lante, as well as a noviciate and a free school for girls. The saint's room on the first floor is open to the public.

29 ST. PAOLA FRASSINETTI

Via del Gianicolo, 4
☏ 066 83 00 875
🚌 870

Paola (Genoa 1809–Rome 1882) arrived in Rome in 1841, and settled with her Dorothean Sisters in the college for girls on the Salita di Sant'Onofrio. St. Paola's room, where her *memorabilia* are preserved, is on the third floor of the Institute.

30 ST. PAUL

Via San Paolo alla Regola, 6
☏ 06 68 80 24 08
🚌 23, 36, 271, 280, 630, 780

According to tradition, the church of San Paolo alla Regola is located in the place where the saint (Tarsus 5–10 AD–Rome 67 AD) lived when he was a prisoner in Rome (Acts 28:30). The house, which was already called the "school of St. Paul" at the time, was used by the Apostle to instruct visitors in the Christian faith.

31 ST. PAUL OF THE CROSS

Piazza dei Santi Giovanni e Paolo, 13
☏ 06 77 27 11
🚌 117

St. Paul (Ovada 1694–Rome 1775), founder of the Passionists, often went to Rome. In 1726, with his brother Giovanni Battista, he went to work at the San Gallicano hospital (Via San Gallicano, 25/A), but he stayed there only two years. He returned to Rome in 1766, having decided to open a convent. In 1770 Pope Clement XIV gave the Passionists the church of Santi Giovanni e Paolo al Celio and the adjoining convent, where St. Paul's room is now a chapel.

32 ST. PETER

Via Urbana, 160
☏ 06 48 14 622
🚌 71

The ancient church of Santa Pudenziana on the Viminal hill rises up on the remains of the house where St. Peter (Bethesda, Galilee–Rome 67 AD) is said to have stayed. The Apostle is venerated in the chapel dedicated to him, to the left of the high altar. The Mamertine prison (Clivio Argentario, 1), where St. Peter, St. Paul and many other Christian martyrs were held, is also open to the public.

33 ST. STANISLAUS KOSTKA

Via del Quirinale, 29
☏ 06 47 44 872
🚌 117

On his arrival from Poland, Stanislaus (Rostkow, Masovia, Poland, 1550–Rome 1568) entered the noviciate of Sant'Andrea al Quirinale. The adjoining convent contains the "Rooms of St. Stanislaus," where he lived until his death.

34 ST. VINCENT PALLOTTI

Via dei Pettinari, 51
🚌 23, 65, 280

St. Vincent was born in Rome, in a house on Via del Pellegrino, and died in Rome in 1850. Between 1837 and 1845 he lived in the convent of Spirito Santo dei Napoletani (Via Giulia, 34), where he was joined by the first brethren of the Society he had founded. In 1846 he moved the community to the church and retreat of San Salvatore in Onda. The "Rooms of St. Vincent Pallotti," where he spent the last years of his life, and a museum of memorabilia, containing his relics, are open to the public.

VATICAN MUSEUMS

PRACTICAL INFORMATION

Vatican City. Entrance on Viale Vaticano.

▪ 06 69 88 38 60.

▪ 49 to the entrance;
23, 81, 492, 990 to Piazza del Risorgimento;
or 62 to St. Peter's.

Ⓜ A Ottaviano.

Opening hours: 9 a.m.–6 p.m. (last admission at 4 p.m.)
Monday through Saturday; 9 a.m.–2 p.m. (last admission
at 12:30 p.m.) last Sunday of the month.

Closed on national and religious holidays.

Special pass needed for the Loggia of Raphael, the
Vatican Library, the Gallery of the Inscriptions and the
Vatican Archives.

Free on the last Sunday of each month.

To visit the gardens,

▪ 06 69 88 40 19.

Tickets can be bought online at www.vatican.va.

A stunning collection of classical and Renaissance art assembled by the Popes in over four centuries of patronage. The palaces that house the collection, and that also include the Sistine Chapel, were the papal residences starting from the 14th century, and were extended with long courtyards built by Bramante in 1503. One of these, the Cortile della Pigna, is named after the bronze pine cone mounted in a niche designed by Pirro Logorio; the pine cone was once part of a Roman fountain dated to the 2nd century AD.

There is a spectacular spiral staircase, designed by Giuseppe Momo in 1932, at the entrance, which leads into the museums. Visitors must follow precise itineraries that can take from at least 90 minutes to at most 5 hours.

The Pinacoteca houses masterpieces on religious themes exhibited chronologically in fifteen rooms. Some of the most important works include the *Deposition of Christ* by Caravaggio, Raphael's *Transfiguration*, an arresting altarpiece by Titian and Leonardo's unfinished *Saint Gerome*.

The museums also host a magnificent collection of Greek and Roman antiquities. The Cortile Ottagono (Octagonal Courtyard) holds the *Laocoön* (1st century BC), a monumental sculpture representing the Trojan priest with his two sons being attacked by serpents, attributed to three sculptors from Rhodes, Agesander, Polydoros and Athenodoros. Discovered in 1506 near the Domus Aurea, it proved a huge influence on many 16th-century Renaissance artists. Also of interest are the sections dedicated to Egyptian, Assyrian and Etruscan artefacts.

The Library was instituted in 1475 by Sixtus IV, who gathered there the many precious collections that had been assembled by his predecessors. It contains interesting manuscripts and volumes and it is also notable from an architectural standpoint and for its decorations. The Galleria delle Carte Geografiche (Gallery of the Maps), 120 meters in length, includes 40 panels made by Ignazio Danti (1580–1583) illustrating the continents as they were known to be at the time.

Raphaels "Stanze" (Rooms)

Raphael was commissioned to decorate the four rooms in the private apartments of Pope Julius II. Work began in 1508 and took more than sixteen years, continuing even after the artist's death. The frescoes, including the famous *School of Athens*, express the religious and philosophical ideals of the Renaissance and are meant to celebrate the triumph of Christian virtues, religion and spiritual truth.

Sistine Chapel

The chapel is named after Pope Sixtus IV who had it built between 1475 and 1483. The chapel was frescoed by some of the most eminent artists of the 15th and 16th centuries. This is the main chapel in the Vatican Palace and the one where the cardinals gather to elect the Pope. In 1481 Perugino, Botticelli, Ghirlandaio, Rosselli, Pinturicchio and Signorelli began work to paint the side walls: to the left, the life of Moses, to the right, the life of Jesus, and 24 portraits of Popes between the windows. In 1508 Pope Julius II summoned Michelangelo to fresco the ceiling, which the artist completed in four years; the three hundred figures that animate the image are of biblical inspiration. Michelangelo later painted the *Last Judgement* on the wall behind the altar, arguably the masterpiece of his artistic maturity.

The contract for the fresco work on the ceiling left the artist free to choose the subjects he painted. During the first year of work these were executed with the help of artists who were pupils of Ghirlandaio; for the following three years, however, Michelangelo preferred to work on his own. The theme he chose was the Creation, while between the lunettes he painted the prophets and the sibyls: a total of 336 sculptural figures in bold colors recently brought back to light. Recent restoration (made public in 1999) indeed revived the outstanding brilliance of the colors of these frescoes. Computers, photographs and spectography also helped to eliminate the effects of successive restorations and bring out the boldness of the original hues from under the film of dirt that had obscured them.

PLACES
OF WORSHIP
OF OTHER
CHURCHES,
RELIGIOUS
COMMUNITIES

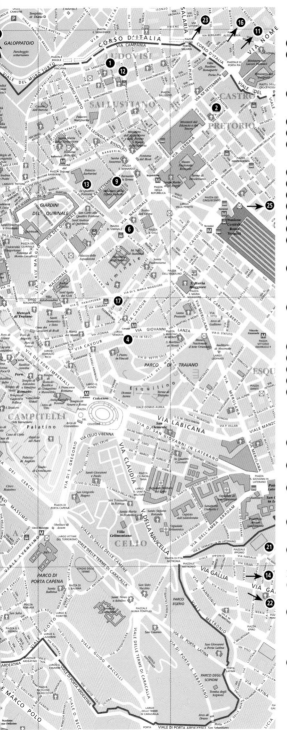

Anglican and American
Episcopalian Churches
(San Paolo dentro le Mura)
5 Via del Babuino, 153/b
6 Via Napoli, 58

Church of Christ
(Seventh-Day Adventist)
24 Lungotevere Michelangelo, 7

Church of Christ
22 Via Messala Corvino, 63
21 Via Sannio, 67
23 Viale Jonio, 286

Baptist Evangelical Church
20 Piazza San Lorenzo in Lucina, 35
16 Via Antelao, 14
18 Via del Teatro Valle, 27
19 Via della Lungaretta, 124
14 Via delle Spighe, 8
15 Via Pullino, 21
17 Via Urbana, 154

Lutheran Evangelical Church
12 Via Sicilia, 70

Church of Scotland
(Presbyterian)
13 Via XX Settembre, 7

Waldesian (Reformed)
and Methodist Church
8 Piazza Cavour, 32
10 Via Banco di Santo Spirito, 3
11 Via Batteria Nomentana, 76
7 Via IV Novembre, 107
9 Via XX Settembre
(angolo via Firenze)

Eastern Orthodox Churches
Egyptian Coptic Church
3 Via San Paolo alla Regola, 6
Greek Orthodox Church
1 Via Sardegna, 153
Russian Orthodox Church
2 Via Palestro, 69
Ethiopian-Eritrean
Community
4 Via Monte Polacco, 5

Salvation Army
25 Via degli Apuli, 42

PLACES OF WORSHIP OF
OTHER RELIGIONS

Jewis Community
26 Lungotevere Cenci

Muslim Community
Islamic Cultural Center and
Mosque of Rome
27 Via della Moschea, 1

EASTERN ORTHODOX CHURCHES

❶ Greek Orthodox Church
Via Sardegna, 153

❷ Russian Orthodox Church
Via Palestro, 69

❸ Egyptian Coptic Church
Via San Paolo alla Regola, 6

❹ Ethiopian-Eritrean Community
Via Monte Polacco, 5

The Eastern Orthodox Churches, whether or not Chalcedonian, take their identity from their claim to a unique uninterrupted link with the traditions of the primitive Church. Their basic unity is guaranteed by their liturgical tradition, and their acceptance of the doctrine of the Trinity, established at the Councils of Nicaea (325) and Constantinople (381). The Greek Orthodox community in Rome dates back to the early 20th century. It had no place of worship of its own until 1955, and depended on the Russian community, which had been established in the mid-19th century. The other communities date from the early 1970s.

ANGLICAN AND AMERICAN EPISCOPALIAN CHURCHES
(San Paolo dentro le Mura)

❺ Via del Babuino 153/b
❻ Via Napoli 58

The Anglican community, which describes itself as "Catholic and reformed," has been present in Rome since 1816. The neo-Gothic church of All Saints (Ogni Santi) was designed by the renowned architect G.E. Street, who also built the American Episcopalian church of San Paolo dentro le Mura (1875). Although these sister Churches are distinct, they both belong to the worldwide Anglican Communion. The usual form of the service is a solemn Eucharist, and they also hold Bible study meetings.

WALDENSIAN (Reformed) AND METHODIST CHURCH

❼ Via IV Novembre, 107
❽ Piazza Cavour, 32
❾ Via XX Settembre (corner of Via Firenze)
❿ Via Banco di Santo Spirito, 3
⓫ Via Batteria Nomentana, 76

The Waldensian Church was founded in 1173 by Peter Waldo as a Church reform movement. At the Synod of Chanforan in 1532, the Waldensians joined the Reform. The Waldensian Theological College was founded in Piedmont in 1855, and moved to Rome in 1922. It has a presbyterian, synodal structure, based on local, regional and national assemblies. Its doctrine is Calvinist

in spirit, based on the Word of God as the only rule of faith and llife. Communion recalls Christ, whose presence is understood as real in a spiritual sense. Baptism is performed according to the rite of the early Church. In 1975 the Italian Waldensians and Methodists came together as the "Evangelical Waldensian-Methodist Church." The Methodist Church grew out of the Anglican Church in England.

LUTHERAN EVANGELICAL CHURCH

⓬ Via Sicilia, 70

The Lutheran Evangelical Church in Italy (CELI) was founded in Rome in 1948 on the initiative of Pastor Dahlgrün, with six other pastors and lay people. In Rome it is represented by a Dean, who is elected every five years. It has a Lutheran, synodal structure, with some variations. The Sunday service is central to the life of the community, with its sermon, prayers and hymns. Lutherans follow the teaching of Martin Luther, founder of the 16th-century Protestant Reformation, and his vision of Holy Scripture as the supreme and sufficient rule of Christian life. The Church is a community in which Scripture is strictly interpreted and the sacraments precisely celebrated, and its central and guiding tenet is the doctrine of justification by faith. Communion is celebrated twice monthly, and it is a reminder that Christ is spiritually present everywhere.

CHURCH OF SCOTLAND (PRESBYTERIAN)

⓭ Via XX Settembre, 7

The British Protestant Church embodies the Puritan strain of Calvinist Protestantism. Historically speaking, it represents a kind of second Reform movement. Its organization is collegiate and based on the Assembly. It promotes ideas of freedom of conscience and tolerance.

BAPTIST EVANGELICAL CHURCH

⓮ Via delle Spighe, 8
⓯ Via Pullino, 21
⓰ Via Antelao, 14
⓱ Via Urbana, 154
⓲ Via del Teatro Valle, 27
⓳ Via della Lungaretta, 124
⓴ Piazza San Lorenzo in Lucina, 35

Baptists draw their inspiration from the sixteenth-century Anabaptists, who proclaimed a radical reform of the Church. The English Baptist mission in Italy began its activities in 1863. In 1920 the Baptist churches joined together as the Italian Evangelical Baptist Union. Their doctrine is similar to that of other Reformed Churches. They practice adult baptism by immersion, and stress the idea of universal priesthood. Local congregations are autonomous and independent, with a regional, national and international collegiate structure that forms the World Baptist Federation. Its purpose is to promote fellowship and solidarity among Baptists from different places.

CHURCH OF CHRIST

㉑ Via Sannio, 67
㉒ Via Messala Corvino, 63
㉓ Viale Jonio, 286

This Church was founded in the United States in 1832, and came to the Rome area in 1949. The Churches of Christ have no ecclesiastical organization, and their local congregations are autonomous. They base their teaching on the Bible, especially the New Testament and its message of Jesus Christ. Believers lead communal prayer, take part in and distribute the Lord's Supper, and can baptize others.

CHURCH OF CHRIST (SEVENTH-DAY ADVENTIST)

㉔ Lungotevere Michelangelo, 7

The Church was founded in America in 1840. Adventists consider Saturday, not Sunday, the Day of the Lord, and live in expectation of Christ's Second Coming. Italy was the first European country in which they preached, and in 1928, the Italian Union (currently Federation) of Adventist Churches was established. Worshippers give much importance to the Bible and to a strict moral life.

SALVATION ARMY

㉕ Via degli Apuli, 42

This is not a church. It is an evangelizing movement founded in London in 1865 to proclaim the Gospel to the city's poorest people. It is organized along almost military lines, to guarantee its effectiveness. It arrived in Italy in 186. It is very open to friendly and cooperative relations with other Christian communities, and turns to the Evangelical Churches for the rituals of baptism and communion.

PLACES OF WORSHIP OF OTHER RELIGIONS

JEWISH COMMUNITY

26 Lungotevere Cenci

The Jewish Community that has existed in Rome since the time of the Maccabees (100–60 BC) is the oldest of the world's Jewish diaspora. Judaism has strong spiritual links with Christianity, since its identity is based on the divine plan of the God of the Coventant. Thus, Jews and Christians share a common spiritual heritage, from the Sacred Scripture of the Old Testament to common liturgical features. The synagogue was built in 1904, when the ghetto was abolished, to replace five scholae or synagogues. It was designed by two non-Jewish architects in Art Nouveau style with Middle Eastern elements. Rome's Jewish community (about 15,000 members) use it very often.

MUSLIM COMMUNITY

27 Centro Islamico Moschea di Roma Via della Moschea, 1

Rome's Islamic community consists of Muslims of many nationalities, all of whom use the large mosque opened in 1995. Islam is the world's second most widespread religion, after Christianity. Its identity focuses on the Koran, the sacred book containing the revelation of the Prophet Muhammad. Muslims believe in the virgin birth of Jesus, and in his miracles, but they do not see him as the son of God. Islam is based on five fundamental pillars: the profession of faith— "There is no God but Allah, and Muhammad is his prophet" (Sura 4, 136); prayer, carried out at prescribed intervals five times a day; alms-giving; fasting; and pilgrimage.

APPENDICES

INDEX OF PLACES

INDEX OF NAMES

ESSENTIAL INFORMATION

Ambulance
[06 57 00.

Carabinieri
[112-06 80 981.

Poison Center
Policlinico Umberto I.
[06 49 06 63.

Health-related Emergencies
[118.

Emergency Medical Service
[06 48 26 741.

Policlinico Gemelli (hospital)
[06 30 54 343.

Police
[113.

City Police
[06 67 691.

Traffic Police
[06 55 441.

E.R. Ambulances
[06 55 10.

Police Headquarters
[06 46 86.

ACI Road Assistance
[116.

Fire Department
[115.

24-HOUR PHARMACIES

Stazione Termini
Piazza dei Cinquecento, 51.
[06 48 80 019.

Internazionale
Piazza Barberini, 49.
[06 48 71 195.

Vaticana
Via di Porta Angelica, 73.
[06 68 64 146.

Opening hours for all pharmacies
[06 22 89 41.

TAXI
[06 39 70.
[06 49 94.
[06 66 45.
[06 88 177.

TRANSPORTATION

AIRPORTS
Aeroporto dell'Urbe
[06 81 20 571.

Ciampino
[06 79 49 41.

Fiumicino
[06 65 951.

ATAC BUSES AND TRAMS

Via Volturno, 65.
[06 46 951.
[167 43 17 84.
[167 55 56 66.

TRAINS
Ferrovie dello Stato
Stazione Termini.
[147 88 80 88.

COTRAL
Via Volturno, 65.
[06 57 531.
[06 43 17 84.
[167 55 56 66.

PHOTOGRAPHIC CREDITS

Archivio Mondadori Electa: Sergio Anelli; Fabrizio Carraro; Giorgio Nimatallah; Antonio Quattrone; Giuseppe Schiavinotto; Arnaldo Vescovo Fabbrica di San Pietro in Vaticano, Vatican City
Foto IAB Musei Vaticani, Vatican City
Opera della Metropolitana, Siena
Osservatore Romano, Vatican City
Luciano Pedicini Archivio dell'Arte, Napoli Soprintendenza speciale per i Beni Archeologici di Roma/Ministero per i Beni e le Attività Culturali Sovrintendenza ai Beni Culturali di Roma Capitale Tips Images, Milan

We wish to thank the Studio Portoghesi for their kind collaboration.

The publisher can be contacted by entitled parties for any iconographic sources that have not been identified.

Front cover: Archivio Mondadori Electa / Arnaldo Vescovo Back cover: Archivio Mondadori Electa/Grzegorz Galazka, Antonio Quattrone, Arnaldo Vescovo

NOTES